"Today's Church finds itself on sh
Nomads helps to calm the quaking
leaders, and unveils a new hope a
within reach of all of us as a sojourner of Jesus."

—LANCE FORD *Author,* The Starfish and The Spirit

"Terry has written a book for those who aren't willing to go back to normal; those who are choosing nomad over normal. In fact, the nomadic life was always supposed to be our normal life as Christ-followers. Don't just read the book, sit at a table with a few other nomads, and let it read you."

—DAN NOLD *Pastor, Calvary Church, State College, Pennsylvania*

"Terry is one of those rare desert fathers we desperately need as we proceed through the dismantling process of the American Evangelical Church. His is a critical voice. Being an unlikely nomad myself, I was in tears more than once as I read the book's affirming words—a must-read for those searching for the church's future."

—RUTH LORENSSON *Coach, Co-Founder, Bridge & Rhino*

"The paths toward new church forms means leaders personally engaged in fresh, new postures and practices, led by vital guides. Terry Walling takes us on a journey, at some points painful, at other hopeful, for what might emerge. Read this book. Let it disturb you and push you towards a hope-filled future for the church."

—KURT FREDRICKSON *Associate Dean, Professional Doctoral Programs, Fuller Theological Seminary*

"Faithfulness is a good and beautiful thing. But sometimes loyalty to the church as we've always known her to be, can actually get in the way of our faithfulness to Christ. Terry gives us permission to step out of the structures that have long held us in place, and offer us a compelling pathway to rediscover the beauty of the Bride of Christ."

—ROB YACKLEY *Co-author of* Thin Places *and the Creator/director of Thresholds*

"In *Unlikely Nomads*, Terry Walling puts words to the experience felt by so many long-time Christians, those who served as the pillars of local churches, until they could do so no longer in good conscience. The decline of the relevance and authenticity of today's churches is a hard reality to accept, but one that Christian leaders need to look in the face. The evangelical church in America is well beyond the point of rebranding. It's time to move to re-inventing. *Unlikely Nomads* is an important book for anyone who wants to find new ways to actually live and function as the church Jesus intended."

—DR. BOB LOGAN *Author of* The Church Planting Journey

"As a skilled mentor, in *Unlikely Nomads*, Terry Walling outlines a compelling case for church leaders to chart a new course with an entirely different destination, for those dissatisfied with the institutional church. Through his stories and examples, Terry models the kind of nomadic guide needed for this sacred journey. *Unlikely Nomads* is for everyone who loves Jesus and longs for more of him in the world."

—ELAINE MAY *Congregational Renewal Leader, Christian Reformed Church in America*

"I kept thinking as I read page after page, Terry had been hearing the voice in my head over many years. He has generously drawn on his deep love for the church, as well as his lifelong experience of mentoring leaders. *Unlikely Nomads* challenges us to potentially be the church Jesus intended, into the future—if it and we are willing."

—REV. PETER WOODS *Anglican Minister, Melbourne, Australia*

"I believe God is using Terry to say something pivotal for each who seek to align with the life of Jesus, today. I challenge each reader and organization to take time to sit, reflect and respond to what is being shared."

—JOEL LAM *Founder/Director, The Breakthrough People*

"Terry calls all unlikely nomads—those who love Jesus and are in pursuit of him but disillusioned with the present construct of the Church—to reimagine what the Church can and should be. Please read it to be challenged and transformed."

—MARVIN WILLIAMS *Pastor Trinity Church, Lansing, Michigan*

"My deep gratitude to Terry Walling for his obedience to 'pay it forward' by writing this pivotal book. *Unlikely Nomads* is a true gift for all those beginning to realize that following the Shepherd to somewhere new requires leaving behind something old."

—KIRK ROMBERG *Executive Coach, Co-Founder, Bridge & Rhino*

"Those who know Terry, and those who do not, are invited to experience God's shaping work in the life of someone committed to hearing God's voice, and following wherever it might lead. This is an essential read for today. But be careful. It could change you."

—JOSH LINDBLOM *Executive Coach and former MLB pitcher*

"Terry has come alongside today's church as she seeks to find herself amid a seismic transition. Like a modern-day prophet, Terry guides the Bride back to the heart of the Groom to live as "apprentices out in the open, together." Church Leaders, be careful picking this book up, you may never come back."

—KEVIN ABBOTT *Associate Director, Union Baptist Association, Houston, Texas*

UNLIKELY NOMADS

IN SEARCH OF THE NEW CHURCH

TERRY B. WALLING

Leader Breakthru Inc.
leaderbreakthru.com
admin@leaderbreakthru.com

Leader Breakthru is a Christian nonprofit dedicated to coaching and resourcing the development of risk-taking, Kingdom leaders who are committed to living, leading and finishing well. For more information and resources, visit leaderbreakthru.com

Cover and interior design: Kyle Walling
Cover artwork: "Landscape with Birch Trees" by Berndt Lindholm (1864)

ISBN 979-8-9892357-0-4 (print)

To Bob and Shirley Trott…

With deep gratefulness for your walks in Christ, and your discipling of so many. Deep thanks to Bob for those early days of showing me what it meant to be discipled. Together, your love and support for Robin and our entire family has meant everything.

You were right all along.
It is about discipleship.

To Dan Nold…

With incredible thankfulness for our shared journey on behalf of the local church, and its leaders. You and Lynn restored our fading hope in the local church in America.

You are right my friend.
Jesus is doing something new in his church.

To the many I have had the privilege to coach and mentor…

With overwhelming appreciation for the openness of your lives, and the chance to learn of how Jesus is at work, birthing something new.

I was right.
I needed you more than you needed me.

CONTENTS

FOREWORD

HUGH HALTER

Terry Walling is one of those rare guides.

He has been my guide for much of my journey, offering me the insights and words of an encouraging father. The book ahead reads more like an ancient treasure hunter's map, hand-penned by one who knows how to guide us to where the treasure, and future is at.

In 2020, my son Ryan passed away at the age of 33.

His life was a road of suffering from his very first day. Five, ten, and sometimes more grand mal seizures every day. Most occurred at night, so Cheryl (my wife) and I never really got a full night's sleep. When they began, I was in seminary but had to leave because his medical expenses and the physical and emotional toll on our family was too high. I lamented having to leave my training for what I thought would be a traditional pastor's lifestyle and calling.

Beyond lamenting I argued with God, I challenged him, and told him I thought it would be more expedient for the building of his church if he would just heal Ryan so we could build with him. His answer was always no. Cheryl and I were left with a huge heart for our lost friends but almost nothing in the tank, and no seminary degree to qualify us for ministry.

Or at least that's how it felt at the time. With the little we had; our home, our living room, some extra beers, some good food, and a couple meals a week, we just started inviting people to be with us. We invited people to the park, our home, our back yard, to tee ball games, hockey games, work parties to build a deck for a friend and so on. We had no salary, and had to work a normal job as a house painter but God built his church. First in Portland, then Denver, and now again in a town called Alton Illinois. It ended up that God's answer wasn't actually a 'no' but more of a 'come… let me show you another way.'

Early on, I felt like no one could understand, and that was partly true. There simply weren't any guides that I could find that had been down our untraditional path of starting or building churches without any of the bells or whistles. In fact, many critiqued and argued and judged our way of life and ministry, and one local leader even suggested to a large ministry network that I was an 'ecclesial anarchist.' Some said, it wasn't really church. Some said, I didn't care about the church and many tried to get us to turn our story into the old church story they came from. But never was Terry one of these. He kept lending his belief in us, and the new work God was doing.

Now 30 years later, I spend time every day listening and coaching, sharing our story to a new breed of ecclesial anarchists who cannot ever go back. None of us really are anarchists. We actually love the church so much we can't just let her mire in the mud of tradition and missiological missteps that are so prevalent and obvious, especially to those outside our ranks. Today, most are still trying to return, post COVID, to a Sunday-centric, speaker-centric, recreational country club way of church. I guess that will always be, and has always been, the wide way. Even though Egypt stripped you of your dignity, its sirens still call you back to 'going to church' one hour a week. But, there is a quiet tidal wave forming of young and old Jesus people alike, that would now do anything to see the church in a new frame, a new light and a new day.

These are today's unlikely nomads, who are now starting to find each other on the trail, and looking for a few leather-skinned missionary sherpas to guide them on this new, but ancient path. Terry is one of those guides.

Read this if you're about to give up.

Give this to a friend who's already given up.

Read it if you haven't given up, but need some finger holds to begin to climb again.

Read it if you are ready to serve and lead and sacrifice everything for God's church.

Unlikely Nomads is not just a book.

It is more like a song you just have to get your friends to listen to.

I pray that Terry's life of listening and loving God's bride, and his daily commitment to lead leaders and serve servants, will become that rare reboot that we all need.

—Hugh Halter
Fellow 'unlikely nomad'

Author of *The Tangible Kingdom, AND: The Gathered and Scattered Church, FLESH,* and *Brave Cities*

"There is no more urgent question for American Christians than this: What is wrong with the American Christian church and how can its witness and ministry be renewed?"[1]

— TIM KELLER

"You don't think your way into a new kind of living. You live your way into a new kind of thinking."[2]

— HENRI NOUWEN

INTRODUCTION

They have left.
They were formerly known as "the committed ones."
The faithful. The leaders. The volunteers.
They were there—every Sunday.

Not attending feels like betrayal.
They stayed until they could stay no longer.

Most would say shedding the Sunday routine, in pursuit of something more, has been the most difficult step they have ever taken in their journey with Christ.

And yet, they have not left Jesus.
Nor have they given up on the Church.

However, they could no longer support the compromised Christianity they see expressed in so many of today's local churches.

Early in their wrestling, they thought *they* were the problem.

They felt isolated from their brothers and sisters, alone in their questioning. In stepping away they have had to confront issues of fear, shame, and guilt.

The Jesus they wanted to follow, was far too often missing in the Sunday equation.

They are on the road now, seeking to return their life back to him and his life.

They are not wandering. They are in pursuit of Jesus, and the life he lived.

They have heard his voice and have made the choice to follow.

They now travel the back roads, encountering others on a similar journey.

They are pilgrims in search of the new church.

These are the "unlikely nomads."

"THE PANDEMIC DIDN'T CHANGE THE WORLD. IT WAS A SIGNAL OF THE CHANGE ALREADY HAPPENING IN THE WORLD."[3]

A CHANGE HAS BEGUN

Many have embarked on a journey toward something new.

What has brought us to this place in time, in terms of the local church, will not be that which takes us into the future. Sometimes you must behave your way into the future.

As we travel beyond this era-ending transition in the life of the local church in America, the dramatic changes that have occurred over the last ten years have served to launch us into a new, and very different period in time. One of unprecedented uncertainty and continuing confusion. It will not soon end.

HOW DO I KNOW?

These types of transition periods happen in the life of the Church, every 500 years, or so (more on that later). And though much continues to change externally in the world in which we live, even more is occurring related to the future of the local church in America.

The problem is that in our haste to return the local church back to what it was pre-pandemic, few have truly taken a step back, and sought to gain a big picture of what Jesus might be at work doing, in his church, from a Kingdom perspective. As Christ-followers, and as the church, we tend to live situationally. But God calls us to live sovereignly. To live above the life that can so easily entangle us. To see all that is occurring from a big-picture point of view, a sovereign mindset.

In the pages ahead, I will challenge each of us to do just that.

To consider all that has happened from the framework of God's, long-term, sovereign work. The question is not whether God has been at work in this moment in time, but rather what has God been at work doing?

"'ONCE MORE I WILL SHAKE NOT ONLY THE EARTH BUT ALSO THE HEAVENS.' THE WORDS 'ONCE MORE' INDICATE THE REMOVING OF WHAT CAN BE SHAKEN—THAT IS, CREATED THINGS—SO THAT WHAT CANNOT BE SHAKEN MAY REMAIN."

— HEBREWS 12:26-27

Dietrich Bonhoeffer found himself in a *shaking* moment.

That now infamous period of time surrounding World War II was also an era-ending transition, a major turning point in world history. It consisted of a world war, cultural upheaval, the rise of hyper-nationalism, and a major turning point in the history of the Church. In these select moments in time, what was, gives way to what is next. Bonhoeffer declared that in these moments, "We must be ready to allow ourselves to be *interrupted* by God."[4]

I believe Jesus has been at work, using these days of uncertainty, to signal an important new work he has begun in his church. It is possible that a major era of the local church has come to an end, and a new one has begun.

As I write in 2023, I am 70 years young.

Sixty of those years have involved my commitment to living out my early faith in Jesus.

Over thirty of those years have been focused on living out my commitment to the local church in America, serving in various capacities: church staff, lead pastor, missions executive focused on church renewal, writing, training, and resourcing. For the last 15 years, I have focused on coaching and resourcing risk-taking, Kingdom leaders who are called to lead the church into greater missional ministry. This last season of my journey has been marked by a time of deep restlessness, uncertainty, confusion, and even isolation. This was compounded as I witnessed all that was transpiring within the American Evangelical Church, and coached many who found themselves in the middle of it.

COULD IT BE THAT THE CHURCH OF TODAY IS NOT THE CHURCH OF TOMORROW?

When the world economy and church shut down in 2020, I was left with time to pray and rethink all that had occurred in my journey over these many years. As the days progressed, and the deadly COVID-19 virus spread across our world, it soon became clear that we were (and continue to be) experiencing a transition far different than the ones most of us have ever experienced. In my study of transitions, I have learned that these times are used by God to show us that we can no longer return to what once was, but at the same time, we are unable to determine which way is forward. The local church in America, and much of the West, is in a major, era-ending, transition.

My goal for this book coincides with my goal for the next years of my life.

I desire to take any, and all, that I have learned, and try to pay it forward to the benefit of the next generation church. More than just documenting my past experiences, my desire is to offer an intersection of past insights with future decisions, as we stand at this crossroads moment in time. We can no longer go back to what the church once was, but the future shape of the church remains unclear. I desire to play some small part in the new, greater work I believe Jesus is doing in the context of the local church.

It is also why, in this junction point in my personal journey, I find myself walking down the roads ahead, as an *unlikely nomad.*

I write for those who find themselves in a transition in relationship to their local church. Many are in their late 30s to 60s, and are struggling. They may be experiencing a diminished passion and weariness after years of attending and faithfully serving in the church. For them, *life in the church* is not what it once was, and with attendance declining across the board, more is being asked of them than ever before. For so long, they have focused their attention on others and ensuring that the doors stay open, that they have forestalled any personal decision-making related to their future in the local church. Though they appreciate the role that it has played in their past, they now recognize their church is at a crossroads.

Like many of you, I continue to remain deeply committed to Christ, and his church. There have always been many outside the church that have questioned its viability. But now, from the inside, many have become disconnected from the church, and some have even developed a new distaste for what the church is seen to represent. The Evangelical Church in America's embrace of partisan politics, and its allegiance to political party over the last few decades, along with its silence in the midst of a series of cultural injustices, have expeditiously alienated an even wider cross-section of churchgoers. All of this points to the need for far more than a simple *rebranding*, or overnight church makeover. Ahead is the need for a major reset of the local church. A time to shed that which is holding the local church back from its primary task of making disciples. Many are resisting the sudden changes that are now upon us. For some, the security of the present, and the church they have always known, blocks the risk they feel is required to discover the new work Jesus has begun to do.

It is important for me to note that personally, this has been a long, sometimes painful, journey. I have given my life for the renewal of the church in America. I have come to these conclusions, often reluctantly, with the recognition that some may feel I have *abandoned ship*, giving up on the existing church. Please know that I still remain deeply committed to the existence and ministry of the local church. Just not in its current expression.

With that, I offer two important confessions before we begin this journey:

First, I offer what's ahead not because I'm an expert on the topics or issues we will discuss. I'm not. What I offer is that which I've been privileged to learn from many who are ahead of me. I desire to sponsor some of the individuals who I have learned from, who have traveled the back roads ahead of us, and share what they have taught me.

Secondly, the focus of these pages is not about predicting the church of the future or introducing a new church model. Instead, our focus is on sustaining the journey ahead, and aligning to the new work Jesus is doing. We will explore paradigms, practices, and spiritual rhythms needed to sustain us as we move forward. At this point, none of us know where we are headed as a Church. Jesus has called us to follow. He will be the one to tell us when we get to where he is taking us. There will come a day when the new wineskins we discover will become the commonplace methodologies of the future, but that day is not this day.

The Apostle Paul reassured the fledgling church that Lydia founded and hosted in Philippi. He penned a promise: "He who began a good work in you will carry it on to completion until the day of Christ Jesus" (Philippians 1:6). I believe this same promise applies to the American church of today. The one who began this good work, is still very much at work.

Ours is the invitation to now follow this same Jesus into a new work, that he has already begun. One that will lead to a new expression of the local church.

Before you decide on what needs to occur in the days ahead…

I invite you to give yourself permission to walk with me down some unlikely roads. Ones we have not walked down before, and consider how Jesus might be at work in his church.

Terry Walling | *June, 2023*

GETTING THE MOST FROM THIS BOOK

In the midst of the era-ending transition surrounding the death and resurrection of Jesus Christ, two early followers of Christ walked the road leading to the city of Emmaus consumed by the events that had just transpired. Some believe the two were Cleophas and his wife, who were so consumed by their conversation, that they failed to recognize Jesus himself joining their intensity. Jesus' explanations and interpretation of the events that had transpired amazed them and transformed their perspective. His words changed their understanding of the narrative. It was equally startling when they realized it was Jesus himself who had been walking with them. Jesus brought definition to the new beginning, and the new place, where they were now headed as his followers (Luke 24:13–32).

We too now travel down a road that is unsettling and unfamiliar, full of many questions and few answers. Our greatest need is to let Jesus back into the conversation. Here are some ways to consider using this book as a resource to potentially recognize his voice better.

YOU

First and foremost, take time to read through the book just for yourself.

There are some personal challenges within these pages that you first need to consider related to your own growth and development. As you read, allow yourself to consider the changes that you are being called to embrace in your own apprenticeship of the life and way of Jesus. Take on a posture of discernment in terms of how God is at work in you. Whatever is happening *in you* is key to what can happen *through you*. Use this as a time of personal reflection and honest self-examination. How is Jesus using this moment in time to do a deeper work in you? What might personal obedience and trust in the days ahead look like for you? Could Jesus be calling you to lay down your past and what you have come to know, in order to follow him more faithfully into the future?

Any change must first take place within you before it can be considered in the lives of others.

YOUR COMMUNITY

We don't get to clarity alone and we don't get to courage without community. Consider using this book as a common read. When read together, it may sow seeds for important conversations that need to occur with others. The journey ahead will be long and will require that we go together, adopt new behaviors, and develop shared practices that yield deeper trust in our King.

As a community, ask yourselves questions like, "What resonates with us? What challenges us the most? What's being reinforced? What's still confusing? What could hold us back?"

As you continue to process the implications of all of this, think about the image of a backpack, specifically one packed for a long climb or extended journey. What from your past may need to be removed from the backpack? What needs to be added for the trip ahead? What could weigh you down as we seek to move forward together?

PERMISSION GROUP

As a community, you may need to grant each other the freedom and permission to interact around the ideas and issues found in this book. A discussion considering a different kind of church can often times feel threatening for those who attend, lead, or minister in local congregations today. In a recent conversation, my good friend, Rob Yackley shared that, "A majority of people who leave their church, in search of a new way of being church, end up in isolation and often with very little faith to hang onto. Processing this transition in the presence of other sojourners feels much healthier." I couldn't agree more.

Consider walking through this book with others as part of a time of learning and discovery, giving permission to each member of the group to process out loud and contribute to the group's learning. Gather periodically to interact around the issues raised, and use the discussion to learn and access other resources. Be free to compare and consider different ideas, and even to disagree with some of the assumptions made in this book. Give yourself permission to invite other voices into the dialogue to share their insights. This format allows you to not only reflect on the concepts raise in this book, but also to become better informed from the learning of others as you consider your own next steps.

"Every transition begins with an ending. We have to let go of the old thing before we can pick up with the new one—not just outwardly, but inwardly."[5]

— **WILLIAM BRIDGES**

NOMADS ARE PASSIONATE, CHRIST-FOLLOWERS, COMMITTED TO THE LIFE AND WAYS OF JESUS.

They are not deconstructing their faith in Christ. Instead, they are following Jesus, and how he is at work, deconstructing today's expression of the local church. One that has been part of the American landscape for many years. Much of the Christianity that nomads see being reflected in the church of today fails to match the life of Jesus. It is why they have taken to the back roads of today's life, pilgrims in search of the new church.

How did we get to this place, and why are we not going back to all of what we have known? These first chapters provide some important background.

Chapter 1… A fable, built upon a familiar narrative.

Chapter 2… A rope unraveling, and now of little use.

Chapter 3… A timeless call for our day, as in the past.

Chapter 4… A look at the life of a nomad, and the days ahead.

CHAPTER ONE

THE PRODIGALS

THE SONG

A fable about a church I once knew.

There was once a generation of travelers who found themselves mired in a time of great unrest. Everything in their day was subject to question. It was an age of discontent. Voices and megaphones drew large crowds of protest. Many found themselves walking amongst the ruins of meaning, resigned to living unwanted lives.

It was during that time that a small number encountered "The Song."

It was a simple song, yet they were captured by its melody. Like many songs sung before, this song was about love. But this song spoke of a different love. The more this song was sung, the more something new occurred. What once seemed dry and judgmental was now offering new life and hope. "The Song" was the "true" love song.

"The Song" was God-breathed, sweeping across the land and into the hearts of many. Those who heard "The Song" joined with

others who were also captivated by its meaning. People were transformed as they lived out the message of "The Song." No song was like it. Its fame spread. With each new day, more sang "The Song."

Concerts of singers now performed it. Worship singers were hired to sing it. Music teachers taught it. Consultants prescribed new ways to benefit from it. Sunday ended up being "the day" for it. Many new versions and recordings of "The Song" seemed to appear everywhere.

Eventually, problems arose. Some tried to make it America's song. Others took "The Song" and departed down self-serving paths. Many set up their tables and sought to sell "The Song." And the further things progressed, the less and less you actually heard the singing of "The Song."

And then, it stopped. The doors of the places where "The Song" was sung were closed. Concerts grew silent. Days turned into weeks. Weeks to months. Some wondered if the simple singing of "The Song" would be no more. When the doors re-opened, the air was not filled with "The Song," but instead with arguments and blame. Many were distracted. Many others demanded "The Song" be sung like before. Many had already begun to drift away. The young wanted no part of the way they now wanted to sing "The Song."

Unknown to most, small pockets of those who had left now traveled down roads with others who felt the same. They decided that nothing was more important than the simple singing of "The Song". Many could have joined them, but most did not. Many wanted what they once had, refusing to accept the common truth that though "The Song" had not changed, the times had. "The Song" was meant to be sung, not just listened to. And, if you listen, you can hear it still being sung. "Lend an ear to a love song... oh a love song... let it take you... let it start."[6]

The *Merriam-Webster Dictionary* defines a fable as, "a fictitious narrative or statement, often a legendary story, seeking to illustrate supernatural happenings." *The Song* is offered as a fable with a spiritual application. One related to the time and the challenges in which we now find ourselves.

The real story of the ending of an era of the local church is illustrated by the fable and lived out in the narrative of our lives. The fable just read draws upon Jesus' use of the "Parable of the Prodigal Son" and the historical narrative surrounding what is known as the "Jesus Movement." The parable of the prodigal tells of the Father's love for his own, and that there is a pathway back for those who have departed. The Jesus Movement of the 1970s, by all accounts, marked a new work of the Holy Spirit that indicated to many that change was coming to the ministry of local churches.

Typically, Jesus' parable of the prodigal son is seen as encapsulating an individual's journey of return; a wayward son returning to the house and love of his father after taking matters of his own life into his own hands. The younger son's posture of genuine repentance and return leads to the father's favor and a joyous celebration. The older brother remaining to serve in his father's house, masked a heart that had wandered away and grown resentful of being left behind to carry on. Though the younger son had wandered far from home, the father's forgiveness was offered and extended to both sons.

One of the first bands to emerge from The Jesus Movement was a band called "Love Song." Chuck Girard, a member of the band, wrote a worship song entitled, "A Love Song," which became one of the anthems of that movement. The opening stanza of the song is included at the end of the fable. The new, fresh expression that The Jesus Movement brought to many lives, and the ministry of local churches, returned the focus of the church back on Jesus and offered new hope to a generation in rebellion.

The potential application of both this parable and this fable offers another important insight into our journey to understand the nomads. Together they offer a call to the local church, particularly in America, to return to a pursuit of the life and message Jesus came to announce. "The Song" and parable speak to a generation of believers, the Baby Boomers, who took the church they inherited from the Builders, into their own hands, and further away from what Christ intended. I'm part of this generation and witnessed this firsthand. The application coincides with the message Jesus has for his church, as penned by the Apostle John. In Revelation 3:16-20, Jesus stands outside of the church of Laodicea, a community known to be lukewarm, "neither cold nor hot."

The Laodicean church considered itself rich, having acquired wealth and not needing anything. Yet, Jesus assessed them as "wretched, pitiful, poor, blind and naked." His call to this church was to "be earnest and repent." Could it be that Jesus' message to Laodicea could also be a message to the church in America today, rich in resources, yet poor and blind when it comes to its current condition?

At best, when measured as a whole, the church in America would be considered lukewarm. At worst, some contend that the vast majority of local churches in America have gone into decline, and become cold to its mandate and command to make disciples. "Just 28% of Christians (within the American Church) are actively involved in any discipleship community."[7] The investment of millions of dollars spent each year, with thousands of clergy staff professionals employed, has resulted in even fewer apprentices of Jesus, who live out the lifestyle and teachings of Jesus. In a nationwide survey of self-identified Christians, one study sought to determine whether Christians have the actions and attitude of Jesus as they interact with others, or if they are more akin to the beliefs and behaviors of Pharisees. Only "14% of today's self-identified Christians—just one out of every seven Christians—seem to represent the actions and attitudes… consistent with those of Jesus."[8]

Though we may each evaluate the state of the church differently, there are very few of us who would struggle to believe that the local church in America stands at a crossroads moment.

"STAND AT THE CROSSROADS AND LOOK; ASK FOR THE ANCIENT PATHS, ASK WHERE THE GOOD WAY IS, AND WALK IN IT, AND YOU WILL FIND REST FOR YOUR SOULS" — JEREMIAH 6:16

I believe that churches can be prodigals. I believe a nation of churches can be seen as a prodigal church. To see ourselves in a collective manner is to finally come to terms with our greatest need—a church that needs to be surrendered back to Jesus.

WHEN WE GIVE THE CHURCH BACK TO JESUS, WE ARE FREED TO FOLLOW HIS LEADERSHIP,

APPRENTICE HIS LIFE, AND ALIGN WITH HIS WORK.

Could it be that we stand on the other side of the door, as Jesus knocks?

If so, the door can only be opened by us. It is only opened by *our own personal* and *corporate surrender*. A choice to return our churches back to Christ.

Jeremiah exhorted the people of God, who were captive to the darkness of their day and at a similar crossroads as we are, to choose "the ancient paths" and "the good way." It is in this way alone that we find "rest for [our] souls" (Jeremiah 6:16).

CHAPTER TWO

THE UNRAVELING

Brian Zahnd, in his book, *Water into Wine*, reflected on the time period known as, The Jesus Movement. "This was a kind of spiritual version of the counterculture movement which swept across the United States and other parts of the world in the early seventies, bringing millions of young people to faith in Christ. The Jesus Movement was the matrix of the Vineyard and Calvary Chapel movements, introducing contemporary worship music to the wider church." [1]

Zahnd goes on to say, "we were young people in our teens and twenties doing life together, hanging out together nearly every night of the week. We had a deep sense that we belonged, not only to Jesus, but to one another."[2]

I lived in Southern California during The Jesus Movement. It was in the 70s.

It was a surreal experience to drive down the busy freeways of Los Angeles, holding up your index finger symbolizing *One Way* to complete strangers in the next car who had a Jesus bumper sticker. And then to have them gesture the same One Way back. In Southern California today, that is not the typical finger you see while on the road.

Calvary Chapel, in Orange County, California, was seen as the epicenter of this new work. My Baptist pastor at the time, warned me that the place with "the big dove" was "off limits for any good Baptist." Being in my teen years that was all the motivation I needed to continue going there! We would sing for the first half of our time on Thursday nights. Then an older bald guy named Chuck Smith, who talked like your comforting grandfather, would teach the Bible for 40 minutes. Tommy Coomes, of the "Love Song" band, often led us in worship. I also remember taking friends to Hart Park in the city of Orange, near my home, to listen to the "Love Song" band sing. Another group, "Mustard Seed Faith," would often join them. Each band member would give testimony to their new life of following Jesus. I also hosted some of those same bands at a "coffeehouse" gathering every Saturday night, which we called "The Bridge."

There was that sense that we all were very much part of something new, exciting, and even revolutionary. God was doing something different, and we were part of that new work. What became known as The Jesus Movement is as close as I have ever come to a true sense of spiritual revival. In the years to come, as it spread across the U.S., this new move of God dovetailed with many different types of local churches seeking a more contemporary approach to ministry. All of this coalesced into something that became known as the "Evangelical Church," the wedding together of charismatic churches, non-charismatic churches, and a diversity of denominations, all loosely knit together by a fresh and clear focus on Jesus.

Fast forward to 2022, a documentary film called *The Jesus Music*, was released giving a chronology of the music birthed during that time. Then in 2023, the release of the feature film, *Jesus Revolution*, highlighted the backstory of The Jesus Movement, and how it came to be. The sudden interest in this period of time brought on a full-blown, Spirit-led, *flashback* for many like me. Those days made an incredibly deep impact on my personal walk with Christ, as well as the thousands who surrendered to Jesus during that time. In new, fresh ways, we witnessed the Holy Spirit at work. The new wine pouring fourth brought with it the need for new wineskins in the established church. Thousands of local churches across America experienced the presence of God, in new ways.

WHAT HAPPENED?

I'm not a historian, anthropologist, or social scientist.

But as a field worker of the local church in America, who labored in the harvest during those years, I began to discover strategic elements of renewal, and a deep personal call to see the local church in America experience new life. I also saw, firsthand, how my generation (Baby Boomers) had taken the reins of the local church and sought to take it to a far different place than where the Builder generation had taken her. In many ways, Boomers tore down many of the staid traditions of the church, seeking to "upgrade" it into a new age, in ways similar to the upgrading of their computers. The newest and latest tech was incorporated into Sunday services. New logos, environments and feel, new programming and worship style. It was all done hoping that the upgrade would create a church that non-Christians would want to attend. In the end, it backfired, resulting in a local church expression that looked (and acted) less like Jesus, and more like the lifestyle preferences of the Boomers themselves. What became known as the "attractional" church, yielded a generation of *attenders* instead of apprentices, who saw *going to church* as their main way of being faithful to Jesus. An unraveling had begun.

Scripture tells how three cords, woven together, are not easily broken (Ecclesiastes 4:12). I find it equally true, that if the three cords or strands of that same rope should begin to fray and unravel, it will begin to lose its strength, integrity, and no longer be able to serve its intended purpose. I believe that the three cords of a rope unraveling provide for us a visual *snapshot* of what has occurred over these past 40 years in the church in America. As a result, today's local church has been weakened, unable to find its feet after a pandemic, left without a prophetic voice, and with fewer and fewer attending. Let's review a short summation of the three ways in which this unraveling has occurred.

THE INSTITUTIONAL UNRAVELING

The Baby Boomer church is the byproduct and reaction to the church of the "Builder" generation (sometimes called the Silent or Greatest Generation). Returning from war, they (the Builders) desired permanence and security. Therefore, they built many of the institutions and organizations that drove the growing economic, social, and political prosperity of the United States that started in the1950s. Many of the institutions, denominations, and traditions of the church in America were solidified and established during that time. The Builders also birthed the largest single generation born in United States history, the Baby Boomers.

The Baby Boomers rejected the forms and style of the Builder church. One built around duty, loyalty, responsibility, rules, and church traditions. Instead, the Boomers focused more on emotions, self-actualization, and the need for meaning. New expressions of worship, relational approaches to evangelism, the rise of expository Bible-teaching that converted Sunday mornings into Bible study classrooms, and even churches residing in drive-in movie theaters and strip malls, all became hallmarks of this new way of doing church. There was also an increasing focus on entrepreneurship, and bringing in the best practices of the business world to help meet the need for a new leadership style in the local church. The CEO pastor-leader was installed, and the birth of "megachurches" was soon the result.

As I transitioned out of my college years, I chose to invest both my relational and leadership skills in helping this new movement of doing church find its way into existing local churches. I soon realized that seeing change come to the local church was no easy task. I became lead pastor of my childhood congregation and saw firsthand how institutional demands can block even the most well-intentioned leader's ability to see the church move forward.

As a result, I rolled up my sleeves, joined a mission organization focused on the revitalization of local churches, and set sail for five years in Australia to do just that. After returning to the U.S. and serving as Executive Vice President for the same organization that sent me *down under*, I founded my own ministry organization focused on coaching and resourcing Kingdom leaders who are called to lead the local church to a new place. Though I have personally seen the sparks of renewal like those early days of The Jesus Movement, and some bushfires of hope flare up in various hot spots in the U.S., they have proven unequal to the task of overcoming the resistance to change that now resides within the American church.

The latest American innovation has been "satellite churches" which continued to allow their churches to grow bigger, but not necessarily better. Church methodology and leveraging technology has often served to mask an overall decline of the local church in America, which began in the early 1990s and continues today. In past decades, some in the church have chosen to turn a blind eye to stories of the character failures of megachurch, CEO-type pastors, the chasing of ambition in new, growing churches, and exposure in the press of corruption and sexual abuse (e.g., the Catholic Church, Southern Baptist Convention, etc.). And these are just the stories we have heard. Those outside the church long ago shook their heads at and rejected today's expressions of the local church.

The *institutional thread* once held the American church together. Denominational labels and church affiliation were seen as important. But those days have long since passed. It is not just the disenchanted youth who have moved on. In an article for Christianity Today, Adam Macinnis stated that "Some of the biggest declines in church attendance over the past three decades have been among adults 55 and older."[3] Savannah Kimberlin, The Barna Group's director of research solutions, further reinforced this by saying, "We can't just blame the young people for the drop in church attendance. People are leaving church from all age groups, and older generations are no exception." The Barna Group has found that "the percentage of people reporting weekly church attendance in America between 1993 and pre-pandemic 2020 reached a high of 48 percent in 2009 then plummeted to 29 percent in 2020."[4]

There is still evidence of some healthy churches, often led by leaders passionate for a viable local church, and living lives focused on Christ and his Kingdom. Many of these churches are what I refer to as "bridging" churches. We will define and highlight these later in the book. But even in some of these "healthy" church settings, the numbers are also in decline.

There is a new category of former church attenders known as *Dones* or the "de-churched." Josh Packard's research reveals that the Dones were once pillars of their respective congregations. In his book, *Church Refugees*, Packard writes: "…more than anything what the de-churched want is a home in the truest sense of the word. A place that's safe and supportive and refreshing and challenging. An identifiable place, embedded in a larger community where they both know and are known by those around them and where they feel they can have a meaningful impact on the world. They long for the same kind of church that we all long for. They desire a church that's active and engaged with the world, where people can bring their full and authentic selves and receive love and community in return."[5] What Packard has said could not be more true. Yet, the Dones and de-churched have concluded that the church they seek can no longer be found in the expressions of the church they once attended.

THE POLITICAL UNRAVELING

While the early days of the 1970s saw the beginnings of renewal as a result of The Jesus Movement, battles began to rage over worship styles, the commitment to the authority of Scripture, and views related to Spiritual Gifts. The launch of the Moral Majority, in the late 70s, began to divert the focus from the supernatural to a growing call for engaging in the politics of America. The focus became selecting political candidates who would enact the reforms and changes that Christians desired to see. If you can't change them, then replace them.

With the voice of Jerry Falwell out in front, the *Evangelicals* soon became a voting block not to be dismissed. Instead of little to no voice in the political conversation, now the church began to be *courted* by even the highest offices. In order to "change the nation" from its ever-growing liberal bias, pastors, local churches, and organizations like Focus on the Family, began to endorse the need to vote specific leaders into office who would side with and legislate according to the church's view of morality. Inserts were put inside Sunday bulletins listing which candidates church attenders ought to vote for and support. Policies, platforms, and party candidates, along with voting records of those for (or against) what these groups felt the church should stand for, was the new thrust for how Christians and local churches should respond to a "declining" and "changing" United States.

What is interesting is the political agenda that Falwell brought to center stage, was actually that which he earlier had condemned. "Falwell's overt political activism in the 70s and 80s marked a dramatic personal reversal. In the 60s, he preached against Christian political activism and engagement. His view then was Christians had only one task and responsibility: to preach God's word of salvation through Christ. But when challenged in the 80s, Falwell repudiated his early teaching as 'false prophecy.' In fact, by that time (the 1980s) he was advocating civil disobedience—were Congress to begin drafting women into military service."[6]

This new focus on politics began to siphon off the direct involvement of churchgoers in meeting the needs of their communities. "Love thy neighbor," seemingly became a forgotten command. For many, voting the right person onto school boards, city councils, and into state and federal offices, was now the best way to bring about significant change. The church's voice grew increasingly silent, especially when it came to local and systemic issues of race, immigration, diversity, violence, gender, and growing tensions related to sexual preferences.

As a result of the abdication of its prophetic voice, in recent years, when faithful followers of Christ have sought to speak up, they are often drowned out by the very politicians the wider church voted into office. Effectively speaking, many seem to believe that politicians now speak on behalf of the church. But the dilemma comes when the politicians that Christians voted into office change their stance as they look to appeal to other constituents and seek reelection.

"THE NET RESULT IS THAT TODAY; WHAT IT MEANS TO BE A 'CONSERVATIVE EVANGELICAL' IS AS MUCH ABOUT THE CULTURE, AS IT IS ABOUT THEOLOGY."[7]

The global transition has also heightened the growing societal problems that continue to unravel (i.e., mental illness, gun violence, homelessness, etc.). But, in the end, the church has made a Faustian bargain, "a pact whereby a person trades something of supreme moral or spiritual importance, such as personal values or the soul, for some worldly or material benefit."[8]

The casualty of this integration of partisan politics into the fabric of the local church has led to a church abandoning its call to a hurting world, and congregations divided down political ideologies: friend against friend, brothers and sisters in Christ choosing to no longer speak. What began as leaders calling the church to take a moral stand, now contributes to the continued polarization and unraveling of the church. "In reality, evangelicals did not cast their vote despite their beliefs, but because of them."[9]

THE ATTRACTIONAL UNRAVELING

The attractional model became the dominant paradigm in the American church for the Baby Boomers. Initially, the "seeker-sensitive" churches were judged to be successful in growing Sunday attendance. But in the end, even those in the forefront, leading this movement, declared the approach unsuccessful in its attempts to make disciples. Pastors Greg Hawkins and Cally Parkinson, authors of the Willow Creek *Reveal* report stated: "For as long as anyone can remember, the only question we knew to ask about the church was, 'How many?' But, 'How many?'—by itself—doesn't completely address what the church is called to do."[10] Cally Parkinson went on to say: "If the activities of the church are all about turning people toward Christ and encouraging them to grow spiritually, why doesn't there appear to be a solid connection between participation in church activities and spiritual growth?"[11] There was no link.

The influence and emphasis of the Church Growth Movement on numerical evaluation, and the continuing focus on attracting more attenders to Sunday worship work against what should be the church's commitment to discipleship. To this day, keeping the seats filled continues to overshadow the calls being made for deeper spiritual formation, and greater emphasis on making disciples. The "attractional model" also serves to reinforce a shallow, inauthentic expression of church that the Millennial and GenZ generations have little interest in attending.

The continuing emphasis placed on *attending* church, as opposed to *apprenticing* the life of Jesus, has now become embedded in the culture: *We have become what we sought to attract.* Said more directly: *What you win them with, is what you win them to.* The Boomers got what they wanted, a church more focused on attracting attenders and gathering a crowd. This approach has netted a generation of church attenders, as opposed to apprentices of Christ. In his book, *The Christian Paradox,* Philip Yancey writes, "The church in America is a mile wide and an inch deep. We have a lot of people attending church services, but many of them have a very superficial understanding of the Christian faith."[12] The Baby Boomers produced a church focused on growing their numbers on Sunday, with little spiritual depth to live out their faith on Monday.

For many years, efforts of rebranding, a new coat of paint, capital campaigns, revamping the website, posting new signage, and updating sound equipment, have been the institutional church's strategy to appeal to new attenders. But now, with some of their most faithful attenders choosing not to return after the pandemic, the viability of the institutional church has been shaken and its ability to survive is endangered. The grand Boomer experiment has broken down and yielded a church struggling to understand which way to go next. The end result is the logical conclusion of these strategies, a generation of attenders, not apprentices. Once again, voices are being heard, but not heeded, as they raise the flag for discipleship and spiritual formation. Meanwhile, fewer and fewer attend.

It is hard for many Boomers to come to terms with the realization that the church we sought to build, and the "big things" we desired to do for Jesus, became only a poor facsimile of the church Christ intended. In the end, we became a church that would describe itself as rich, yet more akin to what Jesus himself depicted as; "wretched, pitiful, poor, blind and naked" (Revelation 3:17). Drama sketches, famous speakers, high-tech instrumentation, streaming broadcasts, high profile megachurches, and a church rich in programming netted fewer and fewer who actually lived the life of Jesus.

A CHURCH FOCUSED ON DISCIPLESHIP, AND APPRENTICING THE LIFE OF JESUS CAN SOMETIMES BE SMALLER IN SIZE, BUT MORE FAITHFUL TO ITS MANDATE.

It has become clear that the American church's ongoing infatuation with crowds, and growing bigger, continues to diminish its ability to fulfill its command to make disciples of Christ.

UNRAVELED

A rope whose cords have separated, whose ends have frayed, and that has long since lost its usefulness, is often discarded. The *unraveling* of the current expression of the American church reveals a church that has lost the vibrancy and vitality it once had. Each chord has been used to illustrate how the local church that many of us grew up in and served, has lost its way and is confused in its purpose. In era-ending transitions, God often reduces the church back to its core purposes. The discarding of the current expressions of the local church should never be interpreted as an abandonment of the local church. Far from it. Rather, this crossroads moment reveals that, for the next generations to experience Jesus and the life he lived in the pages of the Gospels, today, we must be willing to follow the Shepherd in this new work he is doing.

Today will shape tomorrow.

LET'S PAUSE

We all have different views related to the state of the local church in America. Yours may be different than mine, and you may be attending what you consider to be a "good" local church.

IN LIGHT OF THE LAST 5-10 YEARS, CONSIDER THE FOLLOWING:

- What's your take related to how the local church is currently perceived by those outside the church? The culture at large?
- What's your take on the local church being able to prioritize the mandate given to us by Jesus to make disciples?
- What's your take on the church's lack of response to issues of race, injustice, immigration, homelessness, gender issues, abuse, etc.?

Spend some time reflecting.

MY TAKE:

- I believe we are very much in the middle of an unprecedented moment in the history of the local church here in America, an era-ending transition. We are being challenged to realign with the work God is doing and give the church, and its future forms, back to him.
- I believe that Jesus has brought us to the end of ourselves and wants to do a new work. Transitions occur, personally and corporately, to realign us with his intended purposes and take us into something new.
- I further believe that God does some of his greatest work in our lives, and his church, during times of transition.

WHY DON'T WE ASK FATHER ABRAHAM?

CHAPTER THREE

FATHER ABRAHAM

> "We cannot escape most of the crises in our lives, nor should we. In fact, these events frequently provide the energy for movement on our spiritual journey, even when we are stuck along the way … and we ask deeper questions about our own life."[1]
>
> — JANET HAGBERG

In Genesis 12-14, Abram (later to be known as Abraham), found himself in the midst of a defining moment. God issued to him and his household the command to "leave." To walk away from all that he and his ancestors had built, and known. To pack their bags. To take only what they could carry, and go. God's command was not vague or ambiguous. It was a clear call to head out on a journey, to an unknown destination. How can someone leave on a journey, without knowing the destination? It seems illogical, and highly impractical. But that is the story behind Abraham's story, and the one I believe we have inherited today.

The *Abrahamic transition*, chronicled in Genesis 12-22, is the call of one man to deepen his trust and dependence on God. Trust is deepened when we are called to obey. Obedience was something that Jesus himself learned and suffering was his teacher (Hebrews 5:8). The life of a Christ-follower will always include calls for obedience, and the need for greater trust. In times of obedience, we learn that our God is *trustworthy*. It is one thing to say we believe in God. It is another to trust him. Obedience is a choice "to believe something," and to "act as if it is true."[2] Obedience often becomes the tipping point of belief. The old hymn writers were right when they called each of us to: "trust and obey, for there's no other way."[3]

In the paradigm of "lifelong development," God's challenge to Abram was an "Obedience Check." Another Obedience Check will occur when Abram is challenged, by God, to sacrifice Isaac, his only son (Genesis 22:1). God tested Abraham's faith (Hebrews 11:17). God tests our faith. To leave and go on a journey to an unknown destination is challenge enough, but to consider the laying down or loss of something of far greater value would test the limits of anyone's obedience. George MacDonald has stated: "Do you love your faith so little that you have never battled a single fear lest your faith should not be true? Where there are no doubts, no questions, no perplexities, there can be no growth."[4]

Obedience Checks are tools of the "potter." They are used, by God to shape character, deepen dependence, and conform our lives to the image of Christ. J. Robert Clinton, author of the book, *The Making of a Leader*, offers an important insight related to calls to greater obedience. "Obedience Checks may appear to contradict earlier leading; they are not always logical. It is one thing to believe in moments when we understand. It is quite another when we are called to obey in that which seems illogical. Obedience checks do not always hinge on us understanding how God is at work."[5] As illogical as Obedience Checks may seem, there will be times when we are called upon, like Abraham, to obey. I believe that the crossroads moment in which we find ourselves is one of those times. *Abrahamic-type* transitions are daunting. They are era-ending transitions. As one major chapter comes to an end, and another begins, courageous obedience is required. Transitions like these, move the people of God to new places of promise. But they require leaving behind the familiar. They happen more than you might think.

"About every five hundred years, the empowered structures of institutionalized Christianity, whatever they may be at that time, become an intolerable carapace [hard shell] that must be shattered in order that renewal and new growth may occur."[6] The year 2017 marked the 500th anniversary of the Protestant Reformation. In 1517, a small-town Catholic priest named Martin Luther, concerned about biblical inconsistencies within the church, nailed his *Ninety-Five Theses* to the castle church at Wittenberg. In her book *The Great Emergence*, author and religion professor Phyllis Tickle writes of how moments such as this strategically propel the church forward. She calls these moments "era-ending" transitions. They are defining moments where God begins the process of initiating new beginnings, and a next chapter for the Church. When these times of upheaval happen, history shows us that there are always at least three results.

First, a new, more vital form of Christianity does indeed emerge. Second, the organized expression of Christianity which up until then had been the dominant one is reconstituted into a more

> *pure and less ossified expression of its former self. The third result is of equal, if not greater, significance... every time the incrustations of an overly established Christianity have been broken open, the faith has spread—and been spread—dramatically into new geographic and demographic areas, thereby increasing exponentially the range and depth of Christianity's reach, as a result of its time of unease and distress.*[7]

Five hundred years prior to 1517, the Great Schism occurred in 1054.

In short, the Patriarch of the Greek Orthodox Church had Constantinople, while the Pope of the Catholic Church was resident in Rome. One declared Greek as the language of the Church, the other Latin. One used leavened bread in the observance of the mystery of communion and held the key belief that the Holy Spirit proceeds from God the Father. The other used unleavened bread for communion, believed the elements converted into the actual body and blood of Christ (transubstantiation), and added to the Creed that the Holy Spirit proceeds from the Father *and* the Son (filioque). "Two rapidly diverging cultures, two opposing interpretations of the Church and the theology of the Spirit, produced a fracture that is still referred to as the Great Schism. Rome excommunicated Constantinople, and Constantinople returned the favor as it tried to follow Constantine's quest to create a better, purer Rome."[8]

Tickle describes the end of any era-ending moments in the life of the church as a "rummage sale." An ending, where old ways are reformed or abandoned, and a beginning where new forms are free to emerge. For example, the Eastern Church was not destroyed during the Schism, rather "it was freed to become fully itself and fully an expression of its own experience of living out the Christian faith in its own circumstances."[9] The Protestant Reformation was not an extinction event for the Roman Catholic Church, but it did lose its place of dominance socially, politically, and religiously. At the same time, it too experienced a new freedom. It was "freed to weed out its errors and corruptions." As a result of the Reformation, Christianity grew into a global religion whose impact can still be seen in today's globalization that grew out of its "insistence on literacy, which in turn led more or less directly to the technology that enabled world exploration and trade."

> *Christians despair of the upheavals and re-formations that have been the history of our faith—when the faithful resist, as so many do just now, the presence of another time of reconfiguration with its inevitable pain—we all would do well to remember that, not only are we in the hinge of a five-hundred-year period, but we are also the direct product of just such an era. [In times like these, it is important to recall the gains made in the] previous hinge times through which we have already passed.*[10]

The hours Jesus spent in the garden of Gethsemane, before his journey to the cross, ushered in a new era. The ending of what was, is highlighted and emphasized in Jesus' profound prayer: **"Father, if you are willing, take this cup from me; yet not my will, but yours be done"** (Luke 22:42). The cry within his prayer affirms the same struggle that we face to obey, and demonstrates the way forward, which is submission to the will of the Father. His pending suffering, ending in death, meant uncertainty and chaos. But his resurrection and new life brought unparalleled hope.

Simply put: I believe that the political upheaval and polarization that was launched in 2016, the global pandemic, and the continuing issues of worldwide uncertainty, has thrust the American church into an *Abrahamic*, era-ending type transition.

WE ARE AT THE END OF OUR CURRENT EXPRESSION OF THE LOCAL CHURCH, AND AT THE BEGINNING OF SOMETHING NEW.

The question now is not how do we return to where we once were, but rather how do we move forward?

"THE ONE WHO ENTERS BY THE GATE IS THE SHEPHERD OF THE SHEEP. THE GATEKEEPER OPENS THE GATE FOR HIM, AND THE SHEEP LISTEN TO HIS VOICE. HE CALLS HIS OWN SHEEP BY NAME AND LEADS THEM OUT. WHEN HE HAS BROUGHT OUT ALL HIS OWN, HE GOES ON AHEAD OF THEM, AND HIS SHEEP FOLLOW HIM BECAUSE THEY KNOW HIS VOICE." — JOHN 10: 2-4

Jesus' depiction of himself as shepherd, leading his sheep to the new pastures, is the hope of all Christ-followers, especially during the era-ending transition in which we find ourselves. His act of leaving the pen, going out ahead, and calling out those who are his sheep, points to the reality of the Shepherd taking them to a new place. One that is unknown to the sheep, but known to the Shepherd. As they choose to go, they have only his voice to guide them. Like the Obedience Check we saw with Abraham, the sheep's ability to move into the unknown is tied to the voice of the Shepherd. The challenge of the flock is to maintain "voice recognition." How the sheep get to new pastures is directly tied to listening for the Shepherd's voice, *and making the choice to follow.*

New pastures are not found on our own. Rather, only as we surrender to the lead of the Shepherd. The prize of renewed surrender to Christ is revelation (John 5:19-20)—the path made clear. The greater our capacity to hear his voice, the more we are able to gain certainty of his plans. As we obey, he builds our trust, and as our confidence grows in him, so does our ability to trust him further. We are his sheep. He leads. We follow. That is how it has always worked. Not the absence of transitions, but the courage to follow him as he leads us through the times of transitions, and into new pastures.

FOLLOWING ABRAHAM

Sometimes the very things that we want are, in fact, the very things that hold us back. Though I have walked with Christ for many years, I recently found myself confronted with a critical choice, an invitation to obey, like the one given to Abraham.

As the years of my journey with Christ have unfolded, things have often gone very differently than I planned. I became a reluctant pastor, instead of a professional ballplayer. We lived overseas, in Australia as *missionaries* who needed to raise our own financial support, something my wife and I had vowed we would never do. I have taught at the seminary level, something that never existed on my radar. And I became a key leader in a mission organization, something that sent my life in a new direction, far beyond my original goal of becoming a local church pastor. On top of all of that, I ended up writing several books, created many resources for leaders, and trained hundreds of coaches. I share all of that not to show the "notches" on my spiritual belt, but as a testament to the fact that very little of what transpired was part of my initial plan or life goals.

I have also been deeply wounded and greatly loved by fellow Christians. And yet, with all the good that has occurred, late in the game, at seventy years old, I found myself restless for something more.

Over time, I began to realize that I could no longer keep justifying *going to church*, while at the same time, seeing my life exhibit less and less of the behaviors I see in the life of Christ. In truth, I had drifted back from the front lines, and had become an overqualified, *church attender*. As my restlessness continued to grow, the COVID-19 pandemic hit. It was the first time in my life I had ever been told not to go to church. That time of isolation sent me headlong into a personal transition called, the "Finishing Transition." It is a strategic transition for those who are in their 60s-70s, about which I have studied and previously written. It is focused on issues related to finishing well. The questions that arose within me during that time included: Would I keep calling others to finish well, and dare not do that myself? Would I step beyond my current complacency, and realign to the new work I was now seeing Jesus doing in his church? Would I obey to the finish? Or just settle for finishing?

I have spent so much of my life serving the local church, and pouring into and developing its leaders, only to discover that the church itself had become a rival kingdom to Christ's Kingdom in my life. Though I love the church, I love Christ more. I was in need, once again, of surrendering to my "first love." I could no longer keep hoping that the local church in America would someday wake up and change, without first recognizing my own need to repent (rethink) and change. If the church is ever to be relevant to my neighbors who are in search of meaning, I realized that I must first recommit myself to practicing the life I see in Christ. In the quietness of that season, I surrendered my final days, back to him. I became an unlikely nomad.

As hard as it is for me to say, what we call the "local church" today, in most cases, is not at all what Jesus intended for his church. We have misrepresented Jesus to our world in the way we have done church, and often in the lives we have lived. Our challenge today is not related to the validity of or need for, the local church. Rather, it is coming to terms with the failures and shortcomings of our current expression of the church. I have discovered that it is possible, even plausible, to hold to a deep commitment to the local church, but not to the current expression of the church.

WHAT OUR COMMUNITIES, COUNTRY, AND WORLD NEED TO *SEE* AND *EXPERIENCE* IS THE LIFE AND LOVE OF JESUS BEING LIVED OUT.

The preservation of the forms and institutions we have built, the keeping of the doors open, the making sure that the lights are still on, and the staff is paid, will continue to yield fewer and fewer apprentices of the life and way of Jesus. Something has to give. We cannot continue to do the same things and hope for different results.

As it turns out, for years leading up to this point, many others have discovered this for themselves. Feeling what I have come to feel, and arriving at similar conclusions, they themselves have embarked on this same journey. I have found many who also identify themselves as unlikely nomads, also in search of a different, new church, chasing a more genuine expression of the life of Jesus lived out in the context of authentic community. For many years, I remained in the church, trying to promote the need for change. A line was drawn in the sand. Follow Jesus? Or stay in the church? It was time for me to follow down the same path as Abraham: pack my bags, and go.

In Matthew 16:18, Jesus made it clear that he has taken on the responsibility for the building of his Church. To this very day, that continues to be his work. Our responsibility is not to *do something for God*, but to *align with the work God is already doing*. Our call is not to build his Church. Jesus declared, "I will build my church" (Mathew 16:18). The road leading to ambition is built by those who want to do something great for God. The road leading to alignment is one of surrendering to the work he has already begun. Living the life of a nomad in the days ahead is not dissimilar to the one he lived.

Simple? *Yes.* Easy? *No.*

God tested Abraham's faith. God is now testing ours.

BY FAITH ABRAHAM, WHEN GOD TESTED HIM, OFFERED ISAAC AS A SACRIFICE. HE WHO HAD EMBRACED THE PROMISES WAS ABOUT TO SACRIFICE HIS ONE AND ONLY SON, EVEN THOUGH GOD HAD SAID TO HIM, 'IT IS THROUGH ISAAC THAT YOUR OFFSPRING WILL BE RECKONED.' ABRAHAM REASONED THAT GOD COULD EVEN RAISE THE DEAD, AND SO IN A MANNER OF SPEAKING HE DID RECEIVE ISAAC BACK FROM DEATH.
— HEBREWS 11:17-19

We end this chapter with a line that comes from a familiar children's song about Abraham. One that perhaps many of you may have sung in your early years.

The song declares:

> *Father Abraham had many sons (and daughters).*
> *Many sons (and daughters) had Father Abraham.*
> *I am one of them, and so are you.*

In this defining moment, will there be many who follow Abraham's example?

The choice was his.

NOW, THE CHOICE IS OURS.

CHAPTER FOUR

UNLIKELY NOMADS

> "The Road goes ever on and on, down from the door where it began. Now far ahead the Road has gone, and I must follow, if I can, pursuing it with eager feet, until it joins some larger way where many paths and errands meet. And whither then? I cannot say."[1]
>
> — **J.R.R. TOLKIEN**

The movie *Chocolat* depicts the collision of past traditions with the need for new expressions. The storyline is wrapped around a small, fictitious, French village and its ritualistic practice of Lent. It is a story of the battle between a newly arrived shopkeeper wanting to bring about change, and the town's self-appointed gatekeeper, who seeks to keep things as they have always been. Like many movies today, it includes a couple of scenes that are for mature audiences, but allow me to quickly retell the story to help illustrate the realities of the life of a nomad.

The featured character is a mysterious heroine named Vianne, the new shopkeeper, who with her young daughter, moves into the village. She has been led there by a strong northern wind and taken residence in an apartment above a closed-up shop. She transforms the shop into the town's new (and only) "chocolaterie." She and her daughter struggle for acceptance from those in the village, but they have a secret weapon: *chocolate.*

Opening a chocolate shop, during Lent, brings a storm full of tensions to this small town that is predominantly Catholic. The Comte de Reynaud, who also serves as town mayor, is the gatekeeper, the guardian of the way. The Comte role and the traditions it guards have been passed down from generation to generation. But Vianne seeks to break stride with the accepted practices of the past by serving up a mysterious version of chocolate, a recipe of Mayan descent, passed down to her from her father. As brave villagers try this new form of pleasure, they are overwhelmed by its intoxicating flavor, and find themselves wanting more. To make things more interesting, a band of Gypsies show up, docking their wandering boats on shore, near the town. They are not invested in the tensions that are brewing in the town. Johnny Depp plays the part of their leader. He has no interest in the silly practices of the town, or making the investment in long-term relationships, until he meets Vianne.

It was both interesting and beautifully ironic that it was *not the church*, with its newly installed young priest, that called for abstaining from chocolate for Lent. The Priest sought to call the town to the real purpose for the observance of Lent, a renewed focus on God. But the Comte held the line, calling for what had always been done, giving up any form of sweets, especially chocolate, for Lent. He was convinced that what the town had always done, abstaining from sweets, would please God the most.

A groundswell of the villagers made up their minds to no longer comply with the Comte, and a crack began to form in his dam of control. The defining moment comes when the Comte secretly tastes the chocolate and finds himself overcome by its taste and his desire for more. Both he and Vianne soon learn that all of us tend to protect the things we love, but in the end, we are called upon to allow the things we love to change.

My guess is that by now, you see my point for this lengthy illustration. But just in case, let me tease it out for you.

Quite often, it is the people who want the church to remain just as they have always known it to be that hold the church back. Like the Comte, they see it as their duty to preserve that which God used in the past to touch them deeply. But when something new, like the wind of the Spirit, has blown into the church, we can often find ourselves protecting the very thing that Jesus himself is seeking to reform. It is Jesus, not the church that keeps us, "safe and secure from all alarms."[2]

Time and time again, I have coached pastors, church planters, and young leaders raised up by God who were ready to lead, and called to advance the church in their local context, only to hit a blockade of voices protecting what once was. Some of my deepest heartaches as a coach came when I witnessed these leaders and their families torn apart as a result of confrontations with the self-appointed gatekeepers and power brokers of a local church. Politics, infighting, and the protection of the past are not new to the church, but their occurrence has increased as a direct result of the polarization that has taken place over these past several years. Sometimes, it is not the pastor who is holding the church back, but the people themselves.

Chocolat's depictions of Gypsies can help us further understand the life of nomads. Though both nomads and Gypsies are often stereotyped (Chocolat being no exception), they each have distinct ways of living their lives. Gypsies, as we see in Johnny Depp's Roux character, are often depicted as wanderers who move aimlessly from place to place. In contrast, we see Vianne who is in search of something that is authentic and real, a nomad. She longs for a place comprised of people who are honest with one another, and true to themselves.

NOMADS ARE NOT LOST AND WANDERING, NOR ARE THEY AIMLESSLY DRIFTING FROM PLACE TO PLACE. THEY ARE A PEOPLE ON THE MOVE.

Nomads are intentional travelers who live lives of purpose. In earlier days, actual nomads led sheep and livestock to new feeding grounds. In our context and use, "unlikely nomads" are those who once navigated the established highways of the church, but now walk down the roads less traveled. They are not in pursuit of the "perfect church," nor are they chasing freedom from structures or forms, per se. They are not in search of "better worship," or in want of a more dynamic pastor.

THEY ARE IN PURSUIT OF A MORE AUTHENTIC EXPRESSION OF CHURCH.

A church that is focused on living out the life of Christ in the open, shared in the context of community, and better represents his life and way to a skeptical culture.

While most of the church today travels the main roads of accepted practices, nomads are following the winds of the Spirit as it leads them into out-of-the-way places, the small villages, and gatherings, where the life of Jesus is taking root. This journey is not one they had planned. They are following the voice of the Shepherd, as he shapes and instructs them through the people, events, and circumstances they encounter, helping them to discover a better way to live out Christ's Kingdom. The further they go, the more they realize that the new church Jesus is forming is a church that has no walls.

Josh Packard, in his book, *Church Refugees*, provides a stark summation of a millennial he interviewed for the book that was raised attending a local church, but now wants no part of it and is in search of something far different.

> *This model of who has the best advertising, and that it's all about Sunday morning is repulsive to us. My experience is that churches aren't really that different. You either dress up or you dress down, but you go, and there you find an order of service. Generally, there's an opening prayer, announcements, the offering, then 30–40 minutes of preaching, a prayer, and you go home. We wanted relationships that just couldn't be formed, in our experience, in that structure.*[3]

Unlikely nomads make the choice to no longer look to Sunday church attendance as their main form of accountability. They personally take responsibility for their ongoing spiritual growth and seek out community with other nomads, who share like passion and are on the same journey. Though community is not always easy to find, the nomadic life is best experienced with others. Jesus apprenticed his early disciples in the context of community. They learned as they traveled together. They learned his life, as they sought to live out their new lives, in the places and roads on which they traveled.

Jesus very much lived a nomadic life. From his birth in obscurity, to his parents fleeing to Egypt escaping Herod's violent wrath, to his adult years walking the roads of the Galilean countryside. There was no permanent building that he built, and very little of his life was spent in the Temple. He had no address. His life was lived house-to-house, encounter-to-encounter, in smaller-sized groups where deeper intimacy could occur. It was a life lived amongst others, not sustained by the security of a place. It was lived with a day-to-day dependency on the Father: "Foxes have dens and birds have nests, but the Son of Man has no place to lay his head" (Matthew 8:20). And while the life lived by unlikely nomads is not necessarily a call to give up home and shelter, it is a call to no longer be dependent on a church address, but rather to follow and align our lives with Christ.

The New Testament tells of a church that survived not because of the permanence of its buildings, but because of its agility and adaptation to change. As they lived through oppression, attack, and being shamed by the religious leaders of their day, Peter acknowledged that they were "aliens and strangers in the world." He called the early believers to a life of complete dependence on Christ, making the choice to abstain from fleshly desires, "which wage war against your soul" (1 Peter 2:11). Paul sought to remind those in Ephesus that while they may be strangers in this world, they themselves are "...fellow citizens with God's people and also members of his household"

(Ephesians 2:19). Together these two admonitions speak to those who journey as nomads, calling them to both personal holiness and living in accountability to one another.

Sustaining the nomadic life is very different than just attending church on Sunday. It seeks to *be the church* daily as opposed to *going to church weekly*. Nomads are in pursuit of the way of Jesus. They have reaffirmed their lives as his apprentices, longing to experience what they have read about in the pages of the New Testament for themselves. This nomadic life will involve a series of different and likely new behaviors for many of us:

- Living life with Jesus out in the open, both with those who know Jesus, and with those who've yet to meet him. *A church with no walls.*
- Adopting a set of new, spiritual rhythms, out of the need and necessity to deepen one's intimacy with Christ. *Taking personal responsibility for growth.*
- Seeking out others who also desire to apprentice the life of Jesus in their neighborhood or other specific context. *Something far different than just a small group.*
- Giving freedom to the Holy Spirit to lead them beyond their familiar and well-constructed comfort zones. *Challenging many of their self-limiting beliefs.*
- Entering a new level of trust and dependence on God. *Practicing "a long obedience in the same direction."*
- Seeing and embracing the world differently, moving beyond labels, politics, and hidden prejudices. *Learning to live more holistically.*
- Apprenticing the life of Christ by following him back out into the neighborhoods. *Realizing that discipleship occurs as life is lived out.*

This leads us to ask an obvious, and yet crucial question:

"WHY CAN'T ALL OF THIS BE LIVED OUT IN THE CONTEXT AND FORMS OF TODAY'S LOCAL CHURCH?"

The honest answer is that it could. However, having given the last 30 years of my life working alongside the local church to revitalize its ministry, it is becoming increasingly clearer that few churches will be able to make the changes required. The churches that can make these changes are already in the process. But they are the exception, not the rule.

As we close this first section, here is a short summary of why unlikely nomads have set out as pilgrims in search of the new church.

FIRST, NOMADS HAVE COME TO BELIEVE THAT THE CURRENT EXPRESSIONS OF TODAY'S LOCAL CHURCH ARE NOT WHAT JESUS INTENDED FOR HIS CHURCH.

They can no longer keep *going* to church, nor can they be represented by the Christianity coming out of a majority of local churches in America. Nomads have not abandoned their commitment to the local church. But they desire something far different.

Second, nomads accept the reality that they depart on a journey that (as yet) has an unknown destination. They leave not because they are mad, but because they hunger for something more. They believe they have heard the Shepherd's voice, calling them beyond the church they know, and toward the church they have yet to see. Nomads are not chasing a new model or the church of their dreams. Instead, they have chosen to surrender to Jesus and align with the new work he is doing in his church.

Finally, nomads believe we are at a *tipping point*, an era-ending transition in the expression of the local church. Though they are not clear on all that Jesus is at work doing, they know they cannot return to that which once was. It's time to pack their bags, and go.

"UNLESS A KERNEL OF WHEAT FALLS TO THE GROUND AND DIES, IT REMAINS ONLY A SINGLE SEED. BUT IF IT DIES, IT PRODUCES MANY SEEDS." — JOHN12:24

Out of moments of decline, despair, and even death, comes the seeds of something new.

New seeds that have fallen often require a time of winter and dormancy. Covered by a blanket of fallen leaves, new life germinates, as seedlings are fed by the loss and decay of the previous season, reaching toward the promise of the season to come. All that has been, is not lost. Any new beginning is predicated on the ending of what once was.

Ahead are roads we have never walked before.

They will require new ways to think, new guides to help point the way, and new practices needed to sustain us. The remaining chapters seek to equip nomads as they embrace this journey.

The road ahead will be long and off the beaten path. And yet we are following the Shepherd who has called us and leads us to new pastures.

HE LEADS. WE FOLLOW.

POSTURES

THE NOMADIC JOURNEY TAKES US DOWN ROADS SIMILAR TO THOSE THAT JESUS WALKED AS HE TRAINED HIS FIRST APPRENTICES.

Jesus shapes us through life itself. It is not the destination as much as it is the journey. Though the destination and duration of the journey remain unclear, postures (approaches) to the journey help equip those who have chosen the nomadic life to better recognize and follow the voice of the Shepherd.

Postures provoke new insights and provide important guidance for the roads ahead. They also serve as guardrails that help keep each nomad on the paths that lead into the future. Each of the next six chapters highlights one such posture.

HOW DO NOMADS APPROACH THE DAYS AHEAD?

These next chapters help to reframe your paradigms and call you to return to apprenticing the life and ways of Jesus.

The Posture of *Interruption*

The Posture of *Surrender*

The Posture of *Stillness*

The Posture of *Unlearning*

The Posture of *Integration*

The Posture of *Interdependence*

CHAPTER FIVE

THE POSTURE OF INTERRUPTION

> "The great thing, if one can, is to stop regarding all the unpleasant things as interruptions of one's 'own,' or 'real' life. The truth is of course that what one calls the interruptions are precisely one's real life—the life God is sending one day by day."[1]
>
> — C.S. LEWIS

WHY INTERRUPTION?

God does some of his most important work during times of interruptions. Often, we view interruptions as moments that take us away from our "real" life or work, only to find that God is signaling the beginning of something new. Most of us would rather not be interrupted and seek to avoid times of uncertainty and confusion. But God wants into these moments, and seeks to use these encounters to significantly shape our lives and the church.

The Posture of Interruption is a call for nomads to lean into the new work God is doing, and to get all they can out of times of interruption and transition.

ONE HOT, DRY, AFTERNOON, A NOMAD WAS PERCHED HIGH UP ON A HILLSIDE.

He once thought he was destined to rule, but now found himself wondering where it had all gone wrong. No longer was he sitting in a place of esteem and influence, poised to make a great impact and lead others. The only thing he was leading these days were dim, yet compliant sheep, moving them from one pasture to the next, a charge given to him by his father-in-law, Jethro. Nothing in that moment would seem to indicate that he was about to be confronted by a sudden, *divine interruption.*

As he continued to gaze over the arid landscape, and reminisced of the life that once was, he spotted smoke. Not a good sign when herding hundreds of easily distracted sheep. As he looked off in the distance, he could see a large, bushy tree, on fire. As he watched, he noticed that while it continued to burn, it refused to be consumed. The longer this went on, the more the phenomena begged for his attention. As he worked himself, and the flock, over to the area, the fire should have completely consumed the bush, but it had not. It remained ablaze. And then it happened:

"God called to him from within the bush, 'Moses! Moses!' And Moses said, 'Here I am.' 'Do not come any closer,' God said. 'Take off your sandals, for the place where you are standing is holy ground'" (Exodus 3:4-5).

This is one of the most significant, *divine* interruptions in all of Scripture. These are moments when God moves in, and everything we once knew to be true is turned upside-down. Interruptions are often the launch points of personal and organizational transitions. Moses would soon realize that after this moment in time, his life would be forever changed; divinely interrupted in order to discover God's continuing work. "You might think that your woundedness or your sinfulness is the truest thing about you or that your giftedness or your personality type or your job title or your identity as husband or wife, mother or father, somehow defines you. But in reality, it is your desire for God and your capacity to reach for more of God than you have right now that is the deepest essence of who you are."[2]

God confronting Moses at the burning bush presented both a challenge and a choice. Most interruptions do that. Would Moses choose to dismiss all he had just seen as an unexplainable occurrence, of which he would have seen many, given his upbringing? Or would he choose to recognize that this interruption was one of sovereign, divine intervention? Would he choose to accept that God had moved in, or would he choose to move on? Moses removed his sandals, surrendering afresh to the voice of God, accepting all the future changes and challenges this moment would bring for both him and God's people. His standing on that "holy ground" brought the breaking of new ground.

It was a time similar to that of Moses, which occurred in the life of young Samuel. An unknown voice called out to him. His ability to recognize and discern the voice of God forever changed his life. It was also the same for Esther, whose life was suddenly interrupted, turned upside down, and moved into a new role that few thought was hers to occupy. It brought with it the realization that she was born, "for such a time as this." Divine interruptions do that. It was also true for Peter, whose life was first interrupted when he and the others dropped their nets to follow Jesus. He was then further challenged when

Jesus interrupted his plan to return to fishing and called him to feed the sheep of the early Church. Divine interruptions signal the arrival of something far different. It is in these moments that "Abrams" becomes "Abrahams," and "Sauls" are transformed into "Pauls."

God also uses interruptions to shift the Church itself down new paths. Jerusalem was the early epicenter of the Church, only to be interrupted by the outbreak of the Spirit among the Gentiles, in Antioch. The incredible work witnessed by Barnabas moved the church beyond being some sort of Jerusalem-based anomaly, out *unto the ends of the earth*. All this happens because of the changes and challenges that come from interruption.

The life of a nomad must be lived with a Posture of Interruption. Whatever may be ahead is something far different than what we've known, a divine interruption of the paradigms and plans we have for both ourselves and the church. In C. S. Lewis' *Chronicles of Narnia*, the faithful Narnians knew when their lives were being interrupted. Changes were announced by their recognition that Aslan was on the move. "'They say Aslan is on the move—perhaps has already landed.' And now a very curious thing happened. None of the children knew who Aslan was any more than you do; but the moment the Beaver had spoken these words, everyone felt quite different." Lewis goes on: "At the name of Aslan each one of the children felt something jump in its inside."[3]

A look back through church history reveals a church that is not static, but dynamic, and ever-changing. It is we who are a part of the Church that attempt to keep it in the form we most desire. In the end, it becomes staid, and unable to change.

If we were to try and view interruptions from God's perspective, we would soon recognize the ongoing, dynamic, redemptive work of God. The Posture of Interruption reflects our need to continue to surrender to God's sovereign work and live in alignment with his purposes.

Henri Nouwen proclaims the better way, "To wait with openness and trust is an enormously radical attitude toward life ... It is giving up control over our future and letting God define our life."[4] The Posture of Interruption is the call to release our control and embrace a mindset of "discovery" in the now.

HOW OPEN ARE YOU TO BEING INTERRUPTED BY GOD? HOW MUCH ARE YOU WILLING FOR IT TO BE PART OF YOUR JOURNEY AHEAD?

Be careful how you answer...

- Interruptions mean change. Changes to life as you know it or want it to be.
- Interruptions often initiate times of personal transition, moving us from one stage of our development to the next.
- Interruptions often call for a shift in our paradigms. What has helped us arrive at a certain place, may not be the same things that will take us to the next place.
- Interruptions challenge our assumptions of how our life in Christ should be lived, inviting greater alignment with the life and way of Jesus.

The *Moses* reflecting on the hillside soon became a very different *Moses*, called by God to lead his people out of captivity. The nomadic journey is as much about the formational work God is doing in our lives, as it is about revealing the future place he is taking the church. Put simply, instead of chasing a new *form* of church, chase the work God is doing inside of you.

THE FUTURE MUST BE FORGED FROM A REALIZATION THAT WE NOW LIVE IN A DIFFERENT LAND, ARE A PART OF A DIFFERENT WORLD, AND IN NEED OF A DIFFERENT KIND OF FAITH.

One built upon the reality of change and a deeper intimacy with Christ. But, to get there, it'll take the courage to go to a different place, be a different kind of Church, and walk a different path—a path that a transition can often produce.

THE POSTURE OF INTERRUPTION

A divine transitioning to a new place in our journey with God, where his plans and ways, become our plans and ways.

More than anything else, divine interruptions are about forming our character, taking us deeper in our faith and dependence on God. Outward circumstances point to the need for inward development. And, as we are confronted by times of interruption, often more questions than answers surface. Questions arise such as:

- What is my purpose?
- Why can't I shake this restlessness?

- Why do I feel isolated?
- Why all the inconsistencies?
- Why have I lost my passion?
- Why do I keep rehearsing issues and struggles from the past?
- What would happen if I did step out?
- What if I don't have what it takes to step into whatever is next?

Interruptions also go after what is known as the "poser" mentality. A potential mindset that is resident in each of us. Posers are those who have learned the art of pretense, presenting themselves to others as someone, or something they are not. God often interrupts and initiates challenges to our view of *who we truly are* (our identity) and offers a glimpse into *who he truly is* (his character).

Two of the most important paradigms that consistently need to be challenged are: (1) our view of self, and (2) our view of God. Together, they comprise the core of spiritual formation. Interruptions invite us to better understand ourselves, and to see God differently. The net result is a new capacity to see ourselves and know God. "It means a confident, alert expectation that God will do what he said he will do. It is imagination put in the harness of faith. It is a willingness to let God do it his way and in his time. It is the opposite of making plans that we demand that God put into effect, telling him both how and when to do it."[5]

The point is, leaning into times of interruptions creates a greater readiness to recognize and align with the new work God is doing.

HERE ARE SOME QUESTIONS TO HELP YOU CONSIDER YOUR OPENNESS TO DIVINE INTERRUPTIONS:

- Do you have the same willingness to respond to God, as you had when you first put your faith in Christ?
- Do you have so many obligations and responsibilities that you feel a new work of Christ is less and less possible?
- Is there any time to linger with God, listening and opening yourself to Him in new ways?
- Are things planned so tightly that there's little space left to recognize if God were to interrupt?
- As you think about your paradigms shifting and moving into the unknown, what surfaces within you?

Moses' arrival at the burning bush and his interaction with the very presence of God, positioned him to walk through parted seas, and climb Mount Sinai to receive words from God etched on stone. Peter's interruptions, and his willingness to leave what was so known and comfortable, positioned him to lead into the unknown and even an uncomfortable new move of God. You and I must embrace this time of divine interruption, as part of God's ongoing work in each of our lives, and the church. Though the future seems uncertain and even beyond what we can truly grasp, this is our moment to accept God's interruption and embrace the new work that is occurring.

WHAT I HAVE LEARNED...

Interruptions are used by God to launch what is next. God does a transforming work during times of interruption and transitions, that otherwise, we may be unwilling to embrace in the day-to-day. Our role is to get all we can out of these times.

NOMADIC REFLECTIONS

ADOPTING THE POSTURE OF INTERRUPTION HELPS US BE MORE OPEN TO GOD'S TRANSFORMATIVE WORK.

- How has Jesus moved in and interrupted your journey?
- What does it look like to return to a place of absolute surrender and dependence?
- What could this time of interruption mean for the group or community with which you travel?

CHAPTER SIX

THE POSTURE OF SURRENDER

"In the crushing, in the pressing,
You are making new wine.

In the soil, I now surrender,
You are breaking new ground.

'Cause where there is new wine,
there is new power.

There is new freedom,
and the Kingdom is here.

I lay down my old flames,
to carry Your new fire today."[1]

— "NEW WINE," BROOKE LIGERTWOOD

WHY SURRENDER?

The Posture of Surrender means aligning with the new work Jesus is doing in his Church. It is not our Church. It's his. It is not for us to lead, but to follow. As often as we have forgotten and acted otherwise, it has always been that way. What we can say, with certainty, is that ahead of us is something far different than our current expression of church. It is a "rummage sale" and *re-setting* that occurs every few hundred years (see chapter 3).

Ahead are new ways of reflecting and representing the life and way of Jesus to our world. The future of the local church will be lived *out in the open*, together. A church far different than the form we seek to preserve.

In the time of Christ, wine was made through a fermentation process of aging the wine in new, unused wineskins made from the hides of goats or lambs. These new wineskins held the unfermented juice. The juice was left to age for a period of time in the new wineskin. In the fermentation process, gases that are produced give the wine its flavor, color, balance, and distinction. Because the wineskin was new, it could expand and hold the wine, allowing the aging process to be completed. However, if someone poured the same unfermented juice into an *old wineskin*, those same gases would cause the skin to burst. As a result, it would mean the loss of both the new wine and the old wineskin.

NEW WINE REQUIRES NEW WINESKINS.

The crushing of the grapes, and the pressing of that which had been crushed, served as the precursors to the juice being ready for fermentation. The words to the worship song above tell of the "crushing" and the "pressing" being done to the grapes, as the fermentation of the new wine begins. The song speaks to the work being done in the Church today, as well as the work God seeks to do in each nomad. Jesus himself told us that making of new wine brings with it the challenge of change and requires new wineskins (Luke 5:37-38).

New wine has already started fermenting in new wineskins. All across the U.S., many have endured the *crushing* and the *pressing* that has occurred from both inside and outside the church. Many nomads have experienced times of suffering and deep wounding for expressing their questions and dismay over our current forms of church. But there are also nomads who have gone out before us and tell of the appearance and makeup of the new wineskins. These nomads can serve as guides for the road ahead (see section 3).

The current expression of the local church has existed for many decades, virtually remaining the same. Though the music is different, the buildings have changed, the presentation and style have been contextualized, *how* we actually *do* church each week, has essentially remained the same for many hundreds of years. We welcome, sing, announce, and observe the elements, all with one voice teaching the many.

Could it be that after these many years of engaging in a similar approach, with a primary focus on Sunday worship services, we have come to an end of this iteration (wineskin) of the church? Further, could it be that there are things more important to Jesus than just the staging of worship services? Jesus did not come to dictate liturgy, but to invite us to the true, lifelong work of becoming his apprentices.

"THERE IS NO MORE URGENT QUESTION FOR AMERICAN CHRISTIANS THAN THIS: WHAT'S WRONG WITH THE AMERICAN CHURCH AND HOW CAN ITS LIFE AND MINISTRY BE RENEWED?"[2]
— TIM KELLER

The American church seemingly has an overabundance of riches and resources. Even with its talent pool of leaders, its ability to create and innovate, its robust training and theological education programs, and its commitment to mobilize and send more missionaries to more places, we now find ourselves sitting at a crossroads.

My family and I first left our home and the local church I pastored in California, and arrived *down under* in Melbourne, Australia in October of 1988. Our family was the first of a team of four families I had recruited to move with us to Melbourne, to come alongside pastors and leaders, helping to see renewal come to their respective local churches. As our family established ourselves in Melbourne and awaited the arrival of the rest of the team, I began to experience a series of dreams like none I had ever experienced. They pictured my ongoing struggle to gain my father's approval, and his rejection of my decision to move to Australia to help churches, rather than remain as a local pastor. He and my mother were part of the church I had been pastoring in the U.S. The more I experienced the dreams, the more tension built within me. God was clearly signaling my need to address my struggle with seeking the approval of others and was inviting me to look to my heavenly Father for his approval alone.

My plan for those early days, before the others arrived, was to scout out the land, and get ready for the team's arrival. Instead, I found myself in sessions of healing prayer with those skilled in that ministry. I remember incredible times of prayer and healing at Christ Church, Dingley. It began to become clear that God had brought me to "the land down under" for a different reason than my attempt to do a great work *for him*. Rather, I had come *for him* to do a much deeper work *within me.* The question then became, would I allow that to happen? Now, more than thirty years later, I'm glad I made the choice to surrender to his work.

The Posture of Surrender is the laying down of that which we often prize, in order to align with the very work of Jesus. It requires the laying down of our "old flames, to carry [his] new fire today." Surrender is an absolute essential posture of the nomadic life. Imagine the moment when Saul, the "Pharisee of Pharisees," came face to face with the truth that he was actually working against the very one he declared he served. "He fell to the ground and heard a voice say to him, 'Saul, Saul, why do you persecute me?' 'Who are you, Lord?' Saul asked. 'I am Jesus, whom you are persecuting,' he replied" (Acts 9:4-5).

YESTERDAY'S RENEWAL DOES NOT MEASURE UP TO THE CHALLENGES OF TOMORROW.

Surrender is much more than a quick-fix, or small midcourse correction. Former assumptions, yesterday's renewal, and even relying on our inherent skills and natural abilities must now give way to a deeper dependency and realignment with Christ. The coming, new expression of the local church is for those who choose to lay down their kingdoms for His.

The familiar Biblical account of the "Rich Young Ruler" is the story of one who wanted to protect his own kingdom, as he sought to serve Christ (Mark 10:17-27). Though devout in his faith, the rich leader's desire to protect what he had built, and that which offered him security, became a *rival kingdom* to that of Christ's Kingdom. Rival kingdoms come in many forms, besides just monetary wealth. Nomads must empty the *packs-on-their-backs*, and take with them only that which will allow them to better apprentice the life of Christ. Nomads are not *campers* whose RV is loaded up with all the amenities of this life. Nor are they in search of the next thing. They are pilgrims with light backpacks, fully surrendered, in search of the new church. *There is a big difference.*

At the wedding feast at Cana, Mary (Jesus' mother) was informed that the wine had run out. To run out of wine meant disgrace to the host family. The trauma of that moment should not be underestimated, given the lengthy and detailed planning that went into wedding events in those days. Years of harvested grapes had been crushed, barreled, and stored, to produce the fine, aged wine enjoyed on this occasion. Mary's response is worthy of pause and reflection. **"His mother said to the servants, 'Do whatever he tells you'"** (John 2:5).

Mary's counsel for those who were serving at that wedding was not to try to solve this themselves. But rather, *do what he tells you to do.*

Surrender all of your ideas.

Surrender your answers on how to fix this problem.

Surrender how you think things should be done.

Surrender all that you are hiding in your "backpack."

It is telling that John's account notes that it was after the disciples saw Jesus change the water into wine that they truly believed who Jesus said he was (John 2:11). The prize of surrender is revelation.

It was through the writings of Henry Blackaby, and his *Experiencing God* study, that I truly confronted my ongoing need to surrender. For Blackaby, surrender is not necessarily a traumatic event, or a life-and-death emergency, but it is the coming to the end of ourselves. It is what Blackaby refers to as a "crisis of belief" when we cry out, "I don't know what else I can do!"[3] God is far more concerned with who we are, than the tasks we feel called to do. Our cries of desperation signal a deeper need, the need to adopt a posture of surrender.

THE POSTURE OF SURRENDER

The choice to align ourselves with the work that God is already doing, and to more fully trust in *his* right to lead and be in control.

In his book, *Follow Me*, Jan Hettinga shares an account of the ending of World War II. On September 2, 1945, the official Surrender Ceremony of the Japanese Imperial forces to General Douglass MacArthur took place. It was on the deck of the USS Missouri. It was the culmination and end of World War II, but also provides an important picture of all that surrender entails. Hettinga recounts:

> *As the ceremony came to the actual moment of surrender, the Japanese Admiral extended his hand in the familiar gesture of friendship and peace, but General MacArthur refused to take it. He kept his right hand at his side. Sternly he said, 'Sir, your sword first, please.' Then when the defeated Admiral handed over his sword, he extended his hand and grasped the Japanese officer's hand. Why did MacArthur ask for the sword first? Be-*

> *cause the formal disarming of the enemy was the symbol of surrender. Until the weapon was handed over, the hostilities had not formally ceased.*[4]

Each of us holds certain vestiges of our own *kingdoms*. They are kingdoms of control, security, approval, position, power, and past wounding. We hold these tightly like swords by our side, just in case hostilities from our past try to wound us once more. The Posture of Surrender requires that we lay down all we cling to, including those rival kingdoms that we so tightly hold. Whether they involve things we feel we are entitled to, wounds from the past that ought not to have happened, or opportunities that never seemed to come our way—all of these, and more, must be laid down in absolute surrender.

In closing, let me offer three ways that help us live out this Posture of Surrender in the days ahead:

1. CHANGE THE WAY WE APPROACH OUR DAILY LIFE IN CHRIST.

Ours is the task to join the work that Jesus is already doing. Daily we must adopt the practice of aligning with him, and his purposes. Each moment, of each day, we ought to pray: "Jesus, what are you at work doing, and how can I join you in your work?"

2. CHANGE THE WAY WE MEASURE OUR SUCCESS.

His ways and his thoughts are not ours. Like David's years tending sheep, warrior-poets are formed in the hidden valleys and overlooked seasons of life. When no one is watching, when things seem ordinary and so simple, God is often at work shaping and molding us in ways we fail to easily recognize.

3. CHANGE OUR NEED TO SEE IMMEDIATE RESULTS.

Recognize that the journey is lifelong. Things will always return to issues of trust and will always be about embracing his love for us. Dependency builds intimacy. The more we trust him, the more he can trust us.

WHAT I HAVE LEARNED...

The prize of surrender is a greater capacity to see how God is at work. The question is not whether God is at work, but rather do we know how he is at work, and do we have the courage to surrender to that work?

NOMADIC REFLECTIONS

ADOPTING THE POSTURE OF SURRENDER IS THE KEY TO BEING ABLE TO BETTER RECOGNIZE AND UNDERSTAND HOW GOD IS AT WORK.

- Think back through your life and journey in Christ:
- When have you experienced times of genuine surrender?
- What brought you to that point?
- What occurred as you chose to surrender?
- What must be surrendered in the days ahead in order for you to better recognize how Christ is at work?

CHAPTER SEVEN

THE POSTURE OF

STILLNESS

"Just another day in paradise
As you stumble to your bed
Give anything for silence
Those voices ringing in your head

You thought you could find happiness
Just over that green hill
You thought you would be satisfied
But you never will
Learn to be still

We are like sheep without a shepherd
We don't know how to be alone
So we wander 'round this desert
Wind up following the wrong gods home

But the flock cries out for another
And they keep answering that bell
One more starry-eyed Messiah
Meets a violent farewell
Learn to be still
Learn to be still"[1]

— "LEARN TO BE STILL," DON HENLEY & STANLEY LYNCH

WHY STILLNESS?

STILLNESS FOCUSES ON THE ISSUE OF VOICE RECOGNITION.

Following the leadership of the Good Shepherd is tied to our ability to recognize his voice and obey (John 10:4). And yet, too many times, each of us has listened to the voices of strangers (John 10:5) and as the song said, "followed the wrong gods home." The Posture of Stillness is cultivated over time, in ways that counter the noise and static that fills most of our lives. Learning the rhythm of stillness is critical to help nomads stay the course. The hidden strength of any nomad is their ability to hear his "still small voice" (1 Kings 19:11-13 NKJV).

My favorite band is the Eagles—yes, *I am a Boomer.*

I recently reencountered an Eagle's song written by Don Henley, who often places spiritual truths within the songs he writes. "Learn to Be Still is one of these songs that contains a profound truth. As the years have progressed, the noise within my own life has grown. In the midst of a noisy season, I found myself connecting to this familiar song in a new way. What first grabbed me as I listened was that *stillness* was something that must be *learned.* As I made my way deeper and deeper into the lyrics and melody, it felt as if each line, and each note, was taken right from the pages of my own experience. It spoke to a deep longing to leave the noise behind and find a greater stillness within. Whether you're an Eagles fan or not, today's life with all its complexities and busyness cries out for the need to be still.

Before we launch into this chapter, take a few moments, and read again the lyrics of this song. Better yet, if you can, find the song somewhere and listen to it. Allow the lyrics to sink deeper within.

Today, even the most driven, high-capacity individuals are hitting stages of burnout and overload. More and more our go-go-go culture, which celebrates busyness and productivity, is now seeing the relevancy of integrating stillness in our lives. I imagine David to be a similar kind of leader, who sought to follow God down a different path, but who soon realized that stillness was the key to walking the roads ahead.

"BE STILL, AND KNOW THAT I AM GOD."

—PSALM 46:10

The Posture of Stillness has to do with embracing less. Less noise. Less input. Less talking. Less activity. Less useless information. Imagine you're sitting in a coffee shop across from a friend in the midst of deep conversation, only to be interrupted by a barrage of blenders, coffee grinders, background music, and the indiscernible rumble of voices carrying throughout the room. Now imagine you could *flip a switch* and immediately bring silence and stillness to the chaos swirling around you and listen to a friend share something they have never shared before. Though silence may be golden, it is stillness that enables us to truly hear.

Stillness brings with it not only the gift of much-needed quietness to the soul, but also increases the capacity to hear. If we fail to adopt the Posture of Stillness, the pace of life swirling around us will almost certainly drown out the Spirit's magnification of Christ's voice.

Like Elijah learned as he encountered God in a cave, a nomad must learn to detect and recognize God's "still, small voice." It is a voice not heard in the big, the momentous, or even the contrived (1 Kings 19:11-13). We have learned to habitually turn on noise. It has become an automatic reflex when we get into the car, when we go for a jog or walk, and when we are entertaining others. We want noise on when we dine at restaurants, while we shop in stores, and even while we wait on the phone. It is far too easy to put something *on in the background* to placate our constant need for noise. We resist what we call moments of *awkward silence*. Many articles within the National Library of Medicine point to a correlation between our constant need for noise, and deeper struggles related to being alone, lack of contentedness, and negative impact on mental health. One of the most important endeavors a nomad must undertake is learning *how* to be still.

At the core of the Posture of Stillness, are the spiritual disciplines of silence and solitude. These disciplines largely remain untapped by Christ followers today. Most of us gravitate toward the more active types of spiritual disciplines. These two are disciplines of *abstinence*. Many times, Jesus left the crowds who were crying out for more. As Jesus' popularity grew, more than once, he detached himself from the plans and wishes of his disciples. His times alone consisted of cultivating stillness through the practice of silence and solitude (Luke 6:12-13; Mark 6:30-32; Matthew 14:1-13). His stillness prepared him for the future, helped him process grief and struggles, and heightened his ability to "hear the voice of the Father" (John 5:19-20).

HERE ARE SOME DEFINITIONS AND DIFFERENCES BETWEEN SILENCE AND SOLITUDE:

Solitude: The practice of temporarily being absent. Absent from others, and from the many distractions and demands around us. It brings a greater ability to be present with God. It's not a getaway from the demands of people, as much as it is a time of personal restoration in order to better hear and recognize God's voice.

Silence: The practice of voluntarily abstaining from noise. Silence can be done in conjunction with solitude, but can also be practiced as refraining from speaking and sharing, as well as not letting external voices reach us. It allows for a quietening of both the inner, self-conversation, as well as conversations with others. It's about learning to be more at home with God's voice.

Dallas Willard stated that silence and solitude are the most important spiritual disciplines for us to cultivate today. "In our busy, noisy world we need to 'unhook' and get away in order to be alone, and be ourselves with our Lord. Silence and Solitude not only help counteract hectic schedules, but can also be key to help us stay focused, and aligned to the work of Christ. Building more solitude into our daily life takes practice. Over time, you and I can grow more comfortable with being alone with ourselves and our God."[2]

John Ortberg writes about our addictions to noise, activity, and hurry. "Hurry is not just a disordered schedule. Hurry is a disordered heart."[3] In *The Three Movements of Spiritual Life*, Henri Nouwen writes: "Without [silence and] solitude it is virtually impossible to live a spiritual life."[4] He previously said that, "It is a good discipline to wonder in each new situation if people wouldn't be better served by our silence than by our words."[5]

Jesus' invitation to his early disciples seems to be even more applicable for us today: **"Because so many people were coming and going that they did not even have a chance to eat, he said to them, 'Come with me by yourselves to a quiet place and get some rest'"** (Mark 6:31).

For those who now walk the nomadic path, the purpose and end result of stillness is to: **"Let the peace of Christ rule in your hearts, since as members of one body you were called to peace. And be thankful"** (Colossians 3:15). To be sure, the conversation within the church and among her leaders will continue in the days ahead. New ideas as well as new models will be many, as they grasp to find the way forward. The peace of Christ will only come to those who make the choice to stop, be still, and practice the fine art of listening. Richard Foster has said: "The Spirit speaks to us when our heart is still and silent before the Lord—not when we're rushing about and doing our own thing in our own way."[6]

THE POSTURE OF STILLNESS

Making the choice to incorporate silence and solitude into the rhythms of our life, in order to better hear the voice of Jesus.

LET'S PAUSE

For the next 10-15 minutes, let's practice taking on this posture.

HERE ARE THREE TIPS THAT CAN HELP FACILITATE LEARNING TO BE STILL:

1) Begin with a few minutes of quietness, surrendering yourself to God. Allow yourself time to just settle in. Orient yourself to this time by first laying down any struggle you might be carrying, giving it to Christ. Breathing exercises can assist in helping you slow down. You can meditate on Psalm 46:10, "Be still, and know that I am God." Focus on one word at a time from this verse. Let your mind linger on each word for a few seconds before moving on to the next.

2) Now, just sit in quietness and silence. If it still feels awkward, reflect on a time when it was just you and God, and the peace you felt (i.e., out on a boat, a quiet walk around the block, a bike ride in the park, etc.). Allow yourself time and space to just rest in him. If the distraction of other thoughts still invades, write them down, and refocus on just being silent. A "breath prayer," or a single word (such as "Jesus" or "peace") can help you refocus if you find your mind wandering.

3) Grant yourself the freedom to simply rest, without the need to accomplish anything.

In the beginning, 10-15 minutes may seem like an eternity. As you begin to incorporate stillness, you'll find it gets easier, and the duration of your time will increase. The goal is not to "get something" from God, but to rest, and be with him.

ASSUMING THE POSTURE OF STILLNESS IS NO EASY TASK.

Being silent and still can bring on the sense that we are not using our time in a productive manner. Stillness unmasks this distorted view—that we must always be accomplishing something for God—and reveals a deeper desire to see Jesus the same way he sees us, as a friend (John 15:15). Without stillness, the false narrative that we must always be accomplishing something for God goes on and on.

ASSUMING THE POSTURE OF STILLNESS IS CONTRARY TO OUR NATURE.

My natural posture is that of *talking*. When I teach the skills of coaching, I use the acronym WAIT: Why-Am-I-Talking in order to help the coaches remember to listen more and talk less. As I have worked to incorporate more WAIT into my own times of stillness, I have found that it has also naturally found its way into my in-person and online conversations. In a world that beckons me to add my voice to the disarray, I am again reminded of the words of James, "...be quick to listen, slow to speak" (James 1:19).

Desert Spirituality of the 3rd century made silence and solitude more than just a priority. It was a way of life. Their lives in the Egyptian desert often brought minimal provision. They wove and sold baskets to achieve basic levels of sustenance. During the times in which they weaved, they practiced both silence and solitude, along with another discipline of abstinence, fasting. One of the most well-known of these Desert Fathers was Saint Anthony (ca. 251-356), who was born into a well-to-do family. As a young man, he spent long hours meditating on the book of Acts. He was moved by the stories of how the disciples lived the life and way of Jesus. The accounts so impacted his heart that he sold his rights to his parent's estate, gave the money to the poor, and headed out into the desert to seek God.

The book, *The Life of St. Anthony* by Athanasius of Alexandria, is considered one of the most influential writings in Christian history. It depicts how an ordinary man, through solitude and silence, was empowered to live out an extraordinary life, one that many said looked like the life of Jesus. Though I am not necessarily calling us to a radical expression, like those who practiced *Desert Spirituality*, I am calling nomads to make a radical departure from the noise and voices that so permeate our culture, and even the Church, to live a life postured in stillness.

Henri Nouwen reflected: "In solitude, I get rid of my scaffolding: no friends to talk with, no telephone calls to make, no meetings to attend, no music to entertain, no books to distract, just me—naked, vulnerable, weak, sinful, deprived, broken—nothing. It is this nothingness that I have to face in my solitude, a nothingness so dreadful that everything in me wants to run to my friends, my work, and my distractions so that I can forget my nothingness and make myself believe that I am worth something."[7]

A FINAL THOUGHT.

In his book, *The 7 Habits of Highly Effective People,* Stephen R. Covey penned a now familiar illustration, known as "The Big Rock" principle.[8] He tells the story of a professional who was one day speaking to college students. He pulled out a one-gallon, wide-mouthed mason jar, and set it on a table in front of the students. He then produced about a dozen fist-sized rocks and carefully placed them, one at a time, into the jar. When the jar was filled to the top and no more rocks would fit inside, he asked the students, "Is this jar full?"

Everyone in the class said, "Yes." He responded, "Really?"

He once again reached under the table and pulled out a bucket of smaller stone gravel. Then he dumped gravel into the jar, and shook it, causing pieces of gravel to work themselves down into the spaces between the big rocks. Then he smiled and asked the group once more, "Is the jar full?" This time, the class was onto him, and responded: "Probably not!" "Good!" he replied.

He again reached under the table, and now brought out a bucket of sand. He proceeded to dump the sand into the jar, filling the final spaces left between the rocks and the gravel. Once more he asked the question, "Is this jar full?" "No!" the class shouted. Once again, he said, "Good!"

He grabbed a pitcher of water and began to pour it in until the jar was filled to the brim. Then he looked up at the class and asked, "What's the point of this illustration?" One student raised his hand and said, "The point is, no matter how full your life is, if you try really hard, you can always fit some more things into it!" "No," the speaker replied, "That's not the point. The truth of this illustration is this: *If you don't put the big rocks in first, you'll never get them in at all.*"

What's my point in re-introducing this familiar story, especially as it relates to the Posture of Stillness? It is readily acknowledged that it is important for all believers to get away and spend time alone with God. It is seen as important, but seldom practiced. *Stillness* is even more to the point. Though stillness has been widely practiced in the past, it is seldom practiced in the present. Thankfully, spiritual directors and those writing in areas of spiritual formation are once again bringing this practice to our attention. This Posture of Stillness is a "big rock" priority for the nomadic journey ahead, and our capacity to follow Jesus wherever he may lead.

THE LORD SAID, "GO OUT AND STAND ON THE MOUNTAIN IN THE PRESENCE OF THE LORD, FOR THE LORD IS ABOUT TO PASS BY. THEN A GREAT AND POWERFUL WIND TORE THE MOUNTAINS APART AND SHATTERED THE ROCKS BEFORE THE LORD, BUT THE LORD WAS NOT IN THE WIND. AFTER THE WIND THERE WAS AN EARTHQUAKE, BUT THE LORD WAS NOT IN THE EARTHQUAKE. AFTER THE EARTHQUAKE CAME A FIRE, BUT THE LORD WAS NOT IN THE FIRE. AND AFTER THE FIRE CAME A GENTLE WHISPER. WHEN ELIJAH HEARD IT, HE PULLED HIS CLOAK OVER HIS FACE AND WENT OUT AND STOOD AT THE MOUTH OF THE CAVE."
— 1 KINGS 19:11-13

WHAT I HAVE LEARNED...

It is easier to do, but more important to be.

Most of our struggles today are not related to adopting new ideas, or new skills, but rather to cultivating our interior life and developing deeper intimacy with Jesus. In the age of doing, we must embrace the Posture of Stillness as a learned skill. In solitude and silence, we learn to stop producing, stop pleasing people, stop obsessing, and stop solving problems. Rather we learn how to "be still, and know that He is God."

NOMADIC REFLECTIONS

STILLNESS IS REQUIRED TO SUSTAIN THE NOMADIC LIFE. IT IS A "BIG ROCK" PRACTICE THAT MUST BE GIVEN PRIORITY.

As you think about incorporating the Posture of Stillness into your rhythms, utilize these three coaching questions to surface what might hold you back:

- What might keep you from practicing stillness?
- What are you going to do to address this obstacle to practicing stillness?
- What will help ensure that stillness remains a regular part of your spiritual rhythms?

CHAPTER EIGHT

THE POSTURE OF *UNLEARNING*

"All my road is before me, but
All my familiar paths lie far behind me.
My map's here in my hand, but
I have ventured past its tattered edges."[1]

— BRIAN McLAREN

WHY UNLEARNING?

The Posture of Unlearning involves the laying down of our current paradigms and assumptions, in order to adopt new insights and learning needed for the days ahead. The methods and constructs that brought the church here, won't necessarily take us where God is leading.

Taking up the Posture of Unlearning is no easy task.

To *unlearn* requires that we trace our way back to the Age of Enlightenment and look at its impact on our thinking and reasoning today. The Enlightenment was a predominately intellectual movement that occurred between the 1600s and 1800s. Many of our modern ideas, ways of thinking, and scientific discoveries come from the massive shift in paradigms that took place during this time. Three major shifts brought on by the Enlightenment were the focus on *reason*, *individualism*, and *skepticism*. Each of these became central to how they understood life, and how they sought to improve the human condition. Ironically, each of these—reason, individualism, and skepticism—have now become major hurdles in embracing the Posture of Unlearning. The reset required in the days ahead will run cross-purpose to many of the paradigms we have held to be true.

"AS THE HEAVENS ARE HIGHER THAN THE EARTH, SO ARE MY WAYS HIGHER THAN YOUR WAYS AND MY THOUGHTS THAN YOUR THOUGHTS." — ISAIAH 55:9

The Posture of Unlearning is about laying down existing paradigms by which we have viewed our world, the church, and God himself. This enables us to apprentice the life and way of Jesus and become more like the church he intended.

The practice of local churches being led by ordained clergy traces all the way back to the 2nd century of the Church. Many see the commissioning of the *Twelve* and the sending out of the *Seventy* for service as validation for the distinction between clergy and laity. "The Greek word *kleros*, signifying 'share,' or 'inheritance,' is used in I Peter 5:3 to designate the priesthood of all the faithful. Most Christian churches, including the Roman Catholic, understand the clergy as persons functioning within the priesthood of all the people but ordained, or set aside, for particular service, especially in connection with eucharistic ministry."[2] But what if this was never

Jesus' true intent? What if his choice of fisherman, instead of the religious leaders of that day, was an intentional act to place the ministry of the church in the hands of *all* who comprise the church? What if the Eucharist could be offered when we gather together, as family and friends who follow Jesus, as was the case when it was instituted by Jesus himself with the first disciples. What if the future is about us returning to the "priesthood of *all* believers"?

Let these questions just sit here.
We will come back to them at the end of the chapter.

Like most of you, I grew up learning that Pluto was one of nine planets in our solar system. Nine planets, including the Earth, each orbiting around the sun. As kids, we built coat-hanger models of the planets, showing the varied sizes of the planets, each making its path around the sun. We were challenged to remember their names, key facts of their makeup, and what made each distinct as planets. Then, decades later, seemingly out of nowhere, it was declared that Pluto was not a planet.

What? Wait? When did that happen? Who decided that?

No! Pluto is a planet. I learned that in school.

In 2006, the International Astronomical Union (IAU) downgraded the status of Pluto to that of a dwarf planet because it did not meet the three criteria the IAU uses to define a full-sized planet. Essentially Pluto meets all the criteria except one—it has not cleared its neighboring region of other objects. "This means that Pluto still has lots of asteroids and other space rocks along its flight path, rather than having absorbed them over time, like the larger planets have done."[3] So, because it no longer measures up to the agreed-upon criteria, from here and henceforth, there are only eight planets in our solar system: Mercury, Venus, Earth, Mars, Jupiter, Saturn, Uranus, and Neptune. No Pluto!

That's it.

If you hadn't already, you have now officially *unlearned* a truth you thought you knew. You and I were not consulted, asked, or invited to vote whether we agree with this new truth. The decision seems to *violate* how we do things, at least since the Enlightenment in the 1600s. It doesn't really make sense to most of us (reason) to change the game now. But it was decided by a committee locked up in a room without the council of the rest of us (individualism). And, for most of us, the facts presented don't seem compelling enough to make the change (skepticism). I mean really? A "dwarf" planet?

Unlearning is the process of letting go of beliefs, habits, and mindsets that don't match what more recent discoveries have found to be true. Its purpose is to make room for new information and new ways of thinking. It is the "flat" earth giving way to the globe. For believers, it is not about abandoning Biblical imperatives, or no longer holding to the authority of Scripture. It is allowing Jesus to reveal his thoughts, so we might better understand his heart and align with his ways.

THE POSTURE OF UNLEARNING

The sifting and shifting of paradigms, methods, and that which is held to be true, in order to be free to follow Jesus as he leads his Church.

Unlearning, in order to relearn truths about the ways of Jesus, will be an essential part of a nomad's journey. A path similar to the one the early disciples traveled.

The crossing of the Sea of Galilee and the facing of a raging storm set up a classic unlearning incubator. Their *all-hands-on-deck* approach was in stark contrast to Jesus himself asleep in the bow. The experience-born ways these fishermen had learned to cope with and survive the violent storms of the past, were confronted by the paradigms of a new Kingdom.

"THE DISCIPLES WOKE HIM AND SAID TO HIM, 'TEACHER, DON'T YOU CARE IF WE DROWN?' HE GOT UP, REBUKED THE WIND AND SAID TO THE WAVES, 'QUIET! BE STILL!' THEN THE WIND DIED DOWN AND IT WAS COMPLETELY CALM. HE SAID TO HIS DISCIPLES, 'WHY ARE YOU SO AFRAID? DO YOU STILL HAVE NO FAITH?' THEY WERE TERRIFIED AND ASKED EACH OTHER, 'WHO IS THIS? EVEN THE WIND AND THE WAVES OBEY HIM!'" — MARK 4:38-41).

Jesus alluded to this very posture of *unlearning* in the teaching he delivered on the Sermon on the Mount. He began with the phrase, "You have heard that it was said," referring to the popular interpretation of the law. Jesus then declared, "But I tell you," and then he offered a new paradigm and a better way (Matt. 5:17-48). Truth does not change, but how we understand it and how we apply it, does.

Tim Keller calls for the need for shifts in our thinking today, when he declared, "There was no Reformation until there was. There was no revival that turned Methodists and Baptists into culturally dominant forces in the midwestern and southeastern United States—until there was. There was no East African Revival, led primarily by African people, that helped turn Africa from a 9 percent Christian continent in 1900 into a 50 percent Christian continent today—until there was."[4]

The Posture of Unlearning is the call to disentangle some of the thinking, beliefs, methods, and preferences from our past, as well as some of our most treasured traditions that have become enmeshed with the truth of Christ's Kingdom.

UNLEARNING IS THE CALL TO RETHINK ALL OF WHAT WE DO, IN LIGHT OF THE DISCIPLES WE ARE CALLED TO BECOME.

We are following the Shepherd to new pastures, choosing to unlearn, in order that we may better learn to apprentice the ways and life of Jesus.

I am indebted to my friend Mark Sayers and his book, *A Non-Anxious Presence*, for the important perspective related to assumptions we have held to be true, but may now need to be "unlearned." Sayers provides a partial list of accepted assumptions where the Posture of Unlearning must now be applied.[5] It includes:

- Thinking is linear
- Change happens gradually
- More information means more understanding
- Environments remain stable
- Outcomes can be predicted
- Success is tied to efficiency

To unlearn means to honestly examine that which we have come to believe, and why. We see Peter invited into such self-examination and unlearning when he found himself up on a roof and the Spirit declared that which was once forbidden, was now clean (Acts 10:13-16). Sayers observes, the problem we face today is that many of the assumptions that have been embraced by the church, now work *against* the church, as it seeks to engage the culture anew. It is by releasing what once *was* that we open the door and make way for what is to come.

LET'S PAUSE

WHAT DOES THIS IDEA OF UNLEARNING SURFACE WITHIN YOU?

Are there areas in your life, or paradigms you hold to be true, that you sense Jesus may be challenging? What might be your greatest struggle with, or resistance to, unlearning? Reflect for a few moments before moving on.

When you make the choice to live in a different country or culture, you confront the dramatic need for unlearning. In the late 1980s, our family's move from Orange County, California to Melbourne, Australia meant embracing the need to unlearn, in order to learn again. One of the first, and most important ways I began to unlearn, was by choosing to set aside the question, "Why?" In those first couple of months after our arrival, it was all *Why?* questions: *Why* do they drive on the opposite side of the roads? *Why* do our kids have to wear uniforms to school? *Why* is it so hard for leaders to lead? *Why* is it so hard for people in this country to open up? But then it moved deeper.

One day, I went to the local butcher shop to purchase our meat for the week. I entered the shop with a customary, "Hello." "Yank, huh?" the man behind the counter replied. "Yes." I said, feeling my blood pressure begin to rise. I could see where this simple question from the butcher was leading. It was an all too familiar conversation I'd had, over and over again, those first few months.

"I just love you Yanks, and your accent," the butcher continued. I smiled. "Where about in States, mate?" He continued. "Southern California!" I replied. "Ah! I just loved Disneyland! You yanks can sure do it up right." I politely nodded in agreement, paid for my items, and headed out.

When I got home, I was surprised by my strong reaction to what had just happened, as was my wife, Robin. "If one more Aussie tells me that they love my accent, I am going to scream!" All of my pent-up frustration just came rolling out! "Don't they realize that I don't have an accent? *They* have the accent!"

I just stood there, wanting some validation from my supportive wife. "Are you with me on this babe?" I thought. Robin just stood there looking at me, and then quietly said, "You are losing it, Terry! You better go in and lay down!" I realized in that moment that it was time for me to lay down more than my stressed body. It was time to lay down my preoccupation with what once *was*. If I was ever to survive living in this new culture, I would have to unlearn what I had held to be true, and begin to adopt a new way of thinking.

The Posture of Unlearning involves engaging in a new level of humility and making the choice to learn once again. It is often difficult to say the very words that springboard new growth: *"I don't know."*

I close this chapter with a list of some of the paradigms and approaches where the Posture of Unlearning will likely need to be applied in the days ahead:

- *Egalitarian leadership*
  (as opposed to male-dominated)
- *Sovereign formation*
  (as opposed to one-size-fits-all discipleship)
- *Apprenticing*
  (as opposed to attending services)
- *Personal development*
  (as opposed to institutional growth)
- *Long obedience*
  (as opposed to quick fixes and immediate results)
- *Priesthood of all believers*
  (as opposed to clergy-driven systems)
- *Church without walls*
  (as opposed to defined locations)

WHAT I HAVE LEARNED...

What got us *here*, may not *(and often will not)* take us *there*. Unlearning is the call to stay teachable. What served us before is often good, and therefore difficult to lay down. In the beginning, new paradigms and new practices feel awkward, and yet, they are often essential to our next steps in following Jesus.

NOMADIC REFLECTIONS

- Which of your existing paradigms are being challenged?
- Are there certain struggles, right now, that might indicate the need to unlearn?
- What are some ways that Jesus has challenged your thinking/methods/approaches in the past, and invited you to a better, more whole, way?

CHAPTER NINE

THE POSTURE OF *INTEGRATION*

"It would seem that Our Lord finds our desires not too strong, but too weak. We are half-hearted creatures, fooling about with drink and sex and ambition when infinite joy is offered us, like an ignorant child who wants to go on making mud pies in a slum because he cannot imagine what is meant by the offer of a holiday at the sea. We are far too easily pleased."[1]

— C.S. LEWIS

WHY INTEGRATION?

The nomadic journey challenges us to, once again, drop our nets and follow Jesus to an undivided, integrated life. We live fragmented lives in the midst of a fragmented culture. The church has absorbed this disconnected way of life, structuring and separating itself, and its programs, in such a way that believers are not fully formed as apprentices. This has resulted in a misrepresentation of the ways of Jesus to a watching world.

Jesus lived an undivided, integrated life, one that nomads must take up once again.

Brian Zahnd has written a litany of statements that both magnify Jesus' life, and show how Jesus' life reveals the true nature of God. Read through each line slowly.

God is like Jesus.
God has always been like Jesus.
There has never been a time when God was not like Jesus.
We have not always known what God is like—
But now we do.[2]

The use of the word "like" is not meant in a theological sense, but as a description of the practical expression of how Jesus lived his life. Zahnd captures the truth that who Christ is, and how Christ lived his life, represents the exact nature of God. In the same way, our individual lives as apprentices of Jesus, and the collective role of the Body of Christ is to represent the nature and person of Jesus. We are to reveal who Jesus is. Jesus reveals who the Father is.

In seeing the life of Jesus that was lived out, we know the very nature of God. It had not always been so. In Old Testament days, the nature of God was often veiled by the struggles of his chosen people. But Christ came, took on flesh, living an undivided and integrated life for all to see and know. In the Posture of Integration, we are called to represent the life of Jesus—a life lived wholly and in resistance to the fragmentation that surrounds us. In doing so we express Jesus' nature and personhood to the places and people we intersect each day. Integration's purpose extends beyond just the value it brings to our personal journey. Integration is about representation.

Playing off Zahnd's litany, these words can be an anthem for us:

We are to live our lives like Jesus lived.
God has made a way for each of us to express the life of Jesus.
Before the presence of the Holy Spirit,
we were not able to live like Jesus—
But now we can.

Our life of surrender to him, unleashes the Holy Spirit in us to represent Jesus' life to our world.

Nothing has hurt the cause of Christ more than a church comprised of half-hearted, disintegrated believers that offered the world a distorted portrait of the life and ways of Christ, and the nature of our God. It is the portrait that now hangs in many churches and is why many have chosen to walk away. It is also why many more choose not to enter. Our choice to not live an integrated life, has left the most critical question lingering for many: *"Who is Jesus?"*

- Is he the Jesus that is being marketed today by verses on billboards, in multimillion-dollar ad campaigns, and worn on trendy t-shirts?
- Is Jesus' nature like those who stand on the street corners, with signs and megaphones declaring the need to repent, and the impending apocalypse?
- Is he the one behind the "outreach" nights at the church? The carnivals, the giveaways, the bounce houses, and all the other promotions to get people to come to church.
- Is Jesus the one whom megachurch pastors proclaim in their messages, and worldwide broadcasts? Is he the one on the big stage with the lights and fog machines?

- Or is Jesus the American one? His white face and name represented on banners and baseball caps as many stormed the U.S. Capital on January 6, 2020.

WHO IS JESUS?

Most in America have simply moved on, no longer trying to answer this question, or reconcile all that is being said about Jesus, or done in his name. As confused as the watching world might be, those of us who claim to know him seem equally confused about who he is, and the life he calls us to live. Mark Batterson aptly observes, "Most people in most churches think they are following Jesus, but I'm not so sure. They may think they are following Jesus, but the reality is this: they have invited Jesus to follow them."[3]

For nomads, the Posture of Integration is essentially how one commits to faithfully living the entirety of our lives, fully as apprentices of Christ. An integrated life is not a life lived perfectly, but a life lived authentically. Parker Palmer calls the pursuit of integration the journey toward wholeness. Divided is reflective of us. Wholeness is reflective of our God. Love with justice. Judgment with grace. Power with peace. Wholeness. Integration. It is choosing to live a divided life no more, breaking down the walls between what we believe and the ways we choose to behave. How we act, how we treat others, how we neighbor, how we consume, how we love, how we judge, how we sacrifice, how we take responsibility, how we do all of these and much more, integrated around the life of Jesus. Palmer states, "But there can be no greater suffering than living a lifelong lie. As we move closer to the truth that lives within us—aware that in the end what will matter most is knowing that we stayed true to ourselves—institutions start losing their sway over our lives."[4]

THE POSTURE OF INTEGRATION

The expression of the whole life of Jesus, integrated and lived out in our world so as to represent his true nature.

The early apprentices of Jesus were all in. Jesus challenged them to move beyond religious regulations and follow him in living an integrated life. There was no picking and choosing. No à la carte option. Being an apprentice of Jesus meant following with every aspect of their life. Rich Villodas, in his book The Deeply Formed Life, captures the reality of this undivided way saying, "[It] is a life marked by integration, intersection, intertwining and interweaving."[5]

The Posture of Integration exists on both sides of the track; a life equally focused on being and doing. This matches Jesus' calling of his first disciples. "He appointed twelve that they might be with him and that he might send them out to preach and to have authority to drive out demons" (Mark 3:14-15, emphasis mine). Who we are and what we do must be integrated together in order to experience both a deeper intimacy with Christ, and an extended influence for Christ.

THE POSTURE OF INTEGRATION IS COUNTER-CULTURAL, often bringing with it the rejection and doubt of others, especially as we call the church to engage in the more difficult issues of our time.

The values of Christ's Kingdom, when lived out, run counter to all forms of indulgence and self-centeredness, over-consumption and complicity, hatred and inequality, abuse and exploitation ... all too often found first in the church itself. It is for these very reasons that many of the young have walked away from the church.

The Posture of Integration is a call to break free from forms and structures that continue to fuel a compartmentalized faith. It offers a new freedom to begin the journey of knitting our lives in Christ back together. Though many have tried to live out the integrated life while remaining within the current, popular expressions of the church, most have found that the way forward is to break free.

If you are like me, this posture feels pretty overwhelming.

I feel inadequate to live out this way.

I struggle to even recognize the life of Jesus in my own divided life. I often leave times of reflection discouraged by the realization that the fragments of the life I have built are so disconnected from one another and from my faith.

How about you?

Jesus made the choice each and every day to live his life fully surrendered to the will of the Father (John 5:19-20). I have discovered this to be essential in my journey toward greater integration. I have resolved that each day, I must begin by setting my focus on a more integrated life. Each day, "he must increase and I must decrease" (John 3:30 NKJV). Each day I seek to surrender. Each day I ask Jesus to clothe me with an apron of a servant. As simple as this might sound, this practice has increased my capacity to live out a more authentic representation of Jesus.

If the church is to reflect Christ more faithfully in our world, and if we, as his followers, are to make the choice to live more integrated lives as he did, we must give consideration to the following:

1) We can no longer afford to see discipleship as only a classroom event. If we do, it creates a false paradigm related to the truth about discipleship. True discipleship requires both lifelong learning and lifelong living out what is being learned. Apprenticing the life of Jesus cannot occur unless we are actively engaging in mission, taking seriously Jesus' charge to love our neighbor (and even our enemy). Discipleship and mission must be wedded back together. It is how Christ trained his apprentices. For too long, the church (as a whole) has operated under a false belief that a person must first be fully equipped before they are ready to engage in mission. Those who get locked into a never-ending cycle of equipping rarely ever feel equipped enough and as a result seldom integrate it into life. Putting what we have learned into practice is where true apprenticeship happens. Integration comes by behaving our way into becoming like Christ.

2) We can no longer afford to accept the idea that one can apprentice the life of Jesus apart from authentic community. Not just a small group, but a band of fellow nomads, committed to "iron-sharpening-iron," and walking out the ways of Jesus, together. We do not get to clarity alone, nor do we gain courage without community. Jesus taught and

lived in the context of authentic, vulnerable, community. Integration comes by way of the refining fire that burns as we journey together.

3) We can no longer afford to live with a belief that the church can influence and "win" the culture wars by playing the partisan politics game. It is the incarnational life of Christ that changes lives. The church's approach, in recent decades, of putting confidence in the vote—as opposed to Christ's call for us to be peacemakers—has only resulted in dire consequences and increasing polarization. While there are certainly Christians who are called to serve in the political arena, ours is a call to live differently, not vote differently. Integration is an incarnational representation of the life and way of Jesus.

4) We can no longer allow loving our neighbors to mean inviting them to church or a church-sponsored evangelistic/outreach event. Our "neighbors" are not data-points on a church-growth metric. Instead, each apprentice and nomad is called to be a "front-yard" missionary for the sake of their neighbor. Integration is a full expression of Jesus, who taught that the wholehearted love of God must be matched by our wholehearted love of those right next door.

5) We can no longer afford to live with a belief that the issues of the church's past have no relevance or application for us today. The local expression of the church, and the church of America, must address its past as it seeks to live in the present. Issues of racism, violence, rejection, oppression, segregation, power struggles, and many forms of abuse, have all brought about generational pain and resulted in many of the current problems that we face in the church in America.

The church's lack of ownership of its past sin—the wounds and pain of abuse and disenfranchisement—hold it back from faithfully living out Jesus' way in the future. "What is at stake is the credibility and promise of the Christian gospel and the hope that we may heal the wounds of racial violence that continue to divide our churches and our society."[6] Integration is a full expression of Jesus' life and love to all of us, not just a few of us.

6) We can no longer afford to live with a belief that the separation of clergy and lay people, gender-based leadership differences, and even the deep-seated divisions of Eastern and Western church traditions reflect the intent of Jesus for his church. These separations have dramatically held back the church, often prioritizing the preservation of institutional existence over the advancement of Christ's Kingdom purposes. It's time, in so many ways, to complete the Reformation. Integration is the full expression of each person, and each tradition, together, with one voice and one accord, offering glory to Christ (Romans 15:6).

A final thought... the struggle of living a life of integration is a battle each of us fights. It is the battle we fight within. Agnes Gonxha Bojaxhiu, known to the world as "Mother Teresa" served the forgotten, sick, and dying in Kolkata, India. Many would say she offers us a shining example of wholeheartedly living out this Posture of Integration, which is why most of us are baffled by the inner battle she fought.

On Dec. 11, 1979, Mother Teresa, the 'Saint of the Gutters,' went to Oslo. Dressed in her signature blue-bordered sari and shod in sandals despite below-zero temperatures, the former Agnes Bojaxhiu received that ultimate worldly accolade, the Nobel

> *Peace Prize … Yet less than three months earlier, in a letter to a spiritual confidant, the Rev. Michael van der Peet [sic]…she wrote with a weary familiarity of a different Christ, an absent one. "Jesus has a very special love for you,' she assured Vander Peet. '[But] as for me, the silence and the emptiness is so great, that I look and do not see, -Listen and do not hear- the tongue moves [in prayer] but does not speak … I want you to pray for me—that I let Him have [a] free hand."*[7]

WHAT I HAVE LEARNED...

Jesus daily surrendered to the Father, and the Father showed the Son how He was at work (John 5:19,20).

Ours is a call of daily alignment with the work Christ is doing. To live out each day with a faith that permeates every area of our lives. Discipleship, and apprenticing the life and way of Jesus, never stops.

NOMADIC REFLECTIONS

Adopting the Posture of Integration helps each of us better come to terms with, and more fully apprentice, the life of Jesus.

SPEND SOME TIME REFLECTING ON:

- What is your response to the idea of "all-in"—and that of expressing a more fully integrated life?
- How has the environment or culture of your current (or past) church worked both for and against your life looking like Christ's?
- If you feel it would be hard for you (and/or your church) to adopt this posture, what might the implications of that be?

CHAPTER TEN

THE POSTURE OF *INTERDEPENDENCE*

> "They reminded me that Christianity isn't meant to simply be believed; it's meant to be lived, shared, eaten, spoken, and enacted in the presence of other people. They reminded me that, try as I may, I can't be a Christian on my own. I need a community. I need the church."[1]
>
> — RACHEL HELD EVANS

WHY INTERDEPENDENCE?

The Posture of Interdependence runs counter to the "rugged individualism" that has ruled American culture for many decades. It focuses on life being done in the midst of authentic community, where apprentices of Jesus challenge one another in areas of growth and mission. A nomad's ability to sustain the journey ahead requires assuming responsibility for their personal growth and committing to living interdependently.

"Christian community is about gathering and forming of people, and spiritual transformation is about individual and corporate growth, so that they—together— participate in Christ's mission to establish the kingdom of God on 'earth as it is in heaven.'"[2]

Adopting the Posture of Interdependence also means making the choice to move toward greater emotional and spiritual health. It is a commitment to live out a differentiated life, being clear about who we are (and who we are not), and our unique contribution that we offer to others. It is the way nomads can stand separately from each other, and yet journey together. Edwin Friedman, in his book, *The Failure of Nerve*, highlights the important role of differentiation when it comes to living our lives together. "I mean someone who has the clarity about his or her own life goals, and therefore, someone who is less likely to become lost in the anxious emotional processes swirling about... someone who can be separate while remaining connected."[3] Working to bring continuing clarity to one's identity (differentiation) brings a non-anxious presence to any community, and greater potential for growth for all involved.

In contrast, the posture of "independence" is choosing to stand outside the group, preferring one's own commitments and opinions over the shared commitments of the group, which breeds questions and ongoing conflict. While we see in our culture, and often times in the church, a high value placed on independence and stand-out performances of individuals, the loss of connectedness fractures community, and distorts the health and growth of that community. When an unhealthy leader makes the choice to stand alone, outside the group they lead, it is often with the motive of protecting themselves and resisting the level of vulnerability required for authentic community.

The posture of dependence is when we transfer our own personal responsibility for growth on to others. It also serves to distort the effectiveness of any group, as well as halting the maturing process of the individuals within the group, who now become codependent. While there is the reality of healthy dependence on one another for ongoing support and the sharing of resources, churches have often become breeding grounds for codependent relationships. This reality continues to foster a consumer-driven, attender culture within the church. A healthy nomad chooses to journey and live interdependently with others. This involves striking a balance of living life connected to one another while taking responsibility for one's own life and growth. Interdependence allows for relationships within any community to be both healthy and more productive.

All this is to say that each of us must take responsibility for our own apprenticeship of the life and ways of Christ. And it is at this very point, when some make the choice to plateau in their personal growth that life in a community of apprentices can break down. The most tragic expression of this came in the life of Judas Iscariot, who, having lived connected with the other disciples, chose to stand on his own. Though connected in community to the other disciples, his choice to separate himself from them resulted in a betrayal of his apprenticeship to Christ, as well as a deep betrayal of the entire group. Through countless situations, events, and ministry challenges, the twelve stood together, until Judas' choice to stand alone.

There is incredible power in life done together, as was witnessed by the disciples. When four unknown men brought a lame man to Jesus, who was already overrun by the crowds, something happened that, up until that point, had never happened.

"A FEW DAYS LATER, WHEN JESUS AGAIN ENTERED CAPERNAUM, THE PEOPLE HEARD THAT HE HAD COME HOME. THEY GATHERED IN SUCH LARGE NUMBERS THAT THERE WAS NO ROOM LEFT, NOT EVEN OUTSIDE THE DOOR, AND HE PREACHED THE WORD TO THEM.

SOME MEN CAME, BRINGING TO HIM A PARALYZED MAN, CARRIED BY FOUR OF THEM. SINCE THEY COULD NOT GET HIM TO JESUS BECAUSE OF THE CROWD, THEY MADE AN OPENING IN THE ROOF ABOVE JESUS BY DIGGING THROUGH IT AND THEN LOWERED THE MAT THE MAN WAS LYING ON. WHEN JESUS SAW THEIR FAITH, HE SAID TO THE PARALYZED MAN, 'SON, YOUR SINS ARE FORGIVEN.'" — MARK 2:1-5

This storyline has had a deep impact on my personal apprenticeship with Jesus. It reveals for me what Jesus values, his heart for those in need, but also how the religious often seek to thwart his Kingdom work. While you are likely well acquainted with this story, allow me to make a series of observations that could easily be overlooked. I believe each of these helps to illustrate the Posture of Interdependence.

- The four stretcher bearers most likely saw this same man daily, encamped on the paths they traveled.
- The sheer determination and act of these four stretcher bearers signals some sort of motivating factor, beyond what the account tells.
- The names of these four, knowledge of their background, or any facts related to why they chose to act is unknown, and does not seem to be important to the story. All we know is that there were four.
- The fact that the size of the crowd blocked the entrance

to the home says, the religious leaders from nearby towns had crowded out those who needed healing.

- Getting a man, laying on a mat, through the crowds, up onto the roof, and down to the feet of Jesus had to be a difficult task, and something that could only be achieved together.
- Digging/cutting a hole through the thatch, branches, and mud mortar of the rooftop, certainly disrupted the theological discussion taking place between Jesus and the religious elite, who must have been indignant at the intrusion.
- Jesus' response to this interruption is one that acknowledges not just the presence of the four stretcher bearers, but their faith as well.
- In the account, the lame man himself offers no words. Typically, the cries of those in need become the focus of Jesus' attention.
- No other account explicitly tells of Jesus healing one individual because of the faith of others in their community. In this case, the four.
- No other account of physical healing was preceded by Jesus proclaiming the forgiveness of sins in response to the faith of others.
- The crowd was stunned, proclaiming that this was an act they had never seen before.

I have traveled with this story for many years.

It continues to stretch me far beyond the miracle alone. Time and time again, I am struck by the reality that Jesus offered this one who was lame, the forgiveness of sin, and physical healing, because of the faith of others. It was the faith of the four that brought on Jesus' response. This is a theological, out of the box, moment. It was an anomalous act of Jesus, unlike any other recorded. "And when Jesus saw their faith, he said to the paralytic, 'Son, your sins are forgiven'" (Mark 2:6, emphasis mine).

Incredible.

I have come to believe that this encounter demonstrates a profound truth, not only for the healed man, or for the religious leaders, or the crowds who pushed forward to see what had occurred, but also for us. Jesus' intent is for us to do ministry and life together. By affirming these four stretcher bearers, and their collective act of faith, Jesus is signaling that the work of his Kingdom is to be a work done together, interdependently.

Together, the disciples watched the wind and waves obey.

Together, the disciples fed the 5,000.

Together, the disciples went out, two-by-two, to do ministry.

Together, the disciples stayed by Jesus' side, refusing to leave.

Together.

THE POSTURE OF INTERDEPENDENCE

It is in vulnerability of life done together that our faith is refined, clarity is achieved, our identities are shaped, and authentic community is built and sustained.

THE CALL TO WALK A NOMADIC LIFE OFFERS A NEW OPPORTUNITY TO RESET WHAT IT MEANS TO LIVE AS APPRENTICES OF JESUS IN COMMUNITY.

It is something far different than what is often experienced in our current expression of church. Actual nomadic tribes of the past lived in an interdependent relationship with one another, as they dealt with scarce resources and sought to survive life on the road. They often lived in encampments in the countryside, with each member playing an important role in the community. Some of these encampments were made up of individuals from different nationalities, ethnicities, and customs. All who traveled together were counting on each and every member of the group to contribute to the life of the group. Together, they "cut holes" in the "roofs" of the barriers they faced, and obstacles that challenged their survival. Nomadic life then and now, is built upon the strength shared by the many, whose goal was not the survival of one member, but of the whole.

As I shared earlier, in the late 80s, I assembled a tribe of nomads from America, who together made the choice to move to Melbourne, Australia, to serve and resource the churches there. We were apprentices of Jesus who had heard the call to pack our bags, and go, and were ready for our next steps in following him.

Amidst all of the unknowns, we knew what we wanted and committed to doing this together, but in truth had no idea what that really meant. We had each been part of church ministry, small groups, Bible studies, and ministry teams, but soon learned that those did not translate into knowing what it meant to do life together. As we stumbled our way forward, we came face-to-face with our differing expectations of one another, and our misunderstandings regarding the commitment level required for community. Our deep desire for authentic community did not necessarily mean we knew how to live it out. Each of us was drawn into our own refiner's fire, experiencing the good, the difficult, the confusing, and even the wounding from our interdependent lives. Decades later, and even though it was very hard at the time, many of us who were part of that team look back with fondness at the lessons and transformation brought about by this season in community. We who now travel as nomads must come to terms with the need for authentic community. The future church will not be discovered alone, but together.

"LET HIM WHO CANNOT BE ALONE BEWARE OF COMMUNITY. LET HIM WHO IS NOT IN COMMUNITY BEWARE OF BEING ALONE. EACH BY ITSELF HAS PROFOUND PERILS AND PITFALLS."[4]
— DIETRICH BONHOEFFER

The Posture of Interdependence offers two additional insights that we must embrace in order to journey down roads less traveled: We don't get to clarity alone… and we don't get to courage without community.

IN TERMS OF CLARITY ...

Our personal development is a lifelong journey, designed by our creator to be walked together. Assuming the Posture of Interdependence is a commitment to travel alongside one another. Alongside means choosing to listen more, and talk less. Ask more, and solve less. Depend more on the Spirit, and less on our natural abilities. It's about helping one another discover how Jesus is already at work in each of our lives. Whatever we discover, we are more likely to own. Whatever we are told, we more often resist, or question. Clarity comes as you and I discover the answers and take responsibility for their implementation.

By preempting the process of discovery, our answers may bring about greater struggle for those we are trying to help. Though it is often far easier to offer an answer, when we do so, we rob someone of discovery and short-circuit their ownership of change. When Jesus asked the blind man, "What do you want?" he provoked within the man greater ownership of his need for change.

IN TERMS OF COURAGE...

Our personal development is also a journey of challenge, where those who know us well call us to live out our best. It is often not an issue of what we believe, but the courage to live it out, and behave according to what we believe. This is where the "one another" passages in Scripture come into play. Our role in the lives of others who walk the journey of the unlikely nomad is one of serving, honoring, and exhorting one another. There are times when you and I must borrow faith and courage from others.

While we need one another for clarity, we also need one another to possess the courage to live out that which has become clear. It is the sharpening of one another that yields a life and lifestyle that influences others (Proverbs 27:17). It is also in the encouragement that is found within community that we find the courage to live out the life and lifestyle of Jesus.

YOU AND I WILL NOT BE ABLE TO MAKE THE JOURNEY AS NOMADS, ALONE.

Nor will we be able to sustain the journey by living off the growth and insights of others. Self-responsibility and connection to others lend the help we need to continue to walk the roads ahead.

Below is an example of the type of commitments nomads must make to themselves, and to one another, as they take on this Posture of Interdependence:

1) Though the days ahead will be filled with the unknown and untried, I/we choose to go together. To live with a deep resolve to walk alongside one another. To challenge one another to follow the voice of Christ. It is together that we will better learn how to apprentice the life of Jesus.

2) Though we resolve to walk this road with others, I/we also choose to take responsibility for our own personal growth and maturity. I/we personally commit to courageously continue on, even when others become embittered, resentful or abandon our pursuit together.

3) Though we each have our own preferences, strong opinions, and passions for what we think life together should be, I/we commit to not trying to change others, or place demands upon the group. I/we commit to continue to align ourselves with Christ's Kingdom work.

4) I/we commit to living out the sacred call of being apprentices of Christ, extending freedom to others to navigate future roads in the manner I/we each discern is best in order that we may be faithful to Jesus' leading.

WHAT I HAVE LEARNED...

The Posture of Interdependence involves a continued journey toward greater health and a commitment to walk alongside each other, moving into the future together.

NOMADIC REFLECTIONS

ADOPTING THE POSTURE OF INTERDEPENDENCE HELPS US REALIZE THAT WE WERE NEVER INTENDED TO WALK THIS JOURNEY ALONE.

Are you alone in your journey ... or traveling with others?

- *If alone* ... Who do you know that might be like-minded/hearted in their journey?
- *If with others* ... What is working? What's not working? What's missing? What needs to be clarified?

GUIDES

IN THIS NEXT SECTION, WE INTRODUCE GUIDES WHO CAN HELP NOMADS NAVIGATE THE ROADS AHEAD.

They are the *Joshuas* and *Calebs* of our day. Ones raised up by Jesus to help point the way forward. They are living the future, discovering new elements of the new expressions of church.

THE SIX GUIDES WE HIGHLIGHT ARE:

- *Spiritual Entrepreneurs*
- *Curators of the Table*
- *Mentors for Engagement*
- *Architects of Community*
- *Coaches of the Sacred*
- *Conveners of Relationships*

In addition to these six guides, I also give a brief summary of the *Five-fold Leaders* that Jesus has given to the Church as a whole, who provide spiritual oversight and guidance.

A NOTE...

You may be tempted to try to *find yourself* within this list of six guides, but their intent serves a different purpose. Rather than trying to find your role in these new expressions of the church, allow these guides to help you identify the resourcing needed in the coming days. It is by walking with these nomadic guides that we will be better able to discover all that is ahead.

CHAPTER ELEVEN

SPIRITUAL ENTREPRENEURS

"If you want a safe faith, you will never really know God because He doesn't hang out in the shallow end much."[1]

— HUGH HALTER

WHEREVER THE ROADS AHEAD TAKE US...

To move beyond the current forms of the local church, we need those who are already birthing new expressions. New wineskins are needed for new wine.

Spiritual Entrepreneurs are the innovators. They birth the new. They are those among us who have been raised up to help us discover and be part of these new expressions of faith. These guides help give us *eyes to see*, and ways to engage in the new thing that Jesus is already at work doing.

NEW ENVIRONMENTS. NEW FORMS. NEW METHODOLOGIES.

These guides live and minister outside the box. They aid the existing church by forecasting what is ahead and building bridges to what is next. More than that, they serve those who would never come into a local church. They are those who know that the church is (unfortunately) not always a safe place to be or bring others, and act as a source of encouragement and companionship for nomads as they journey onward.

PROFILE

Spiritual Entrepreneurs are artists who are in tune with the work Jesus is doing, painting with new words, new ideas, and creating new environments. They are expressionists who help to reveal Jesus' heart and help expose us to what is next. They are gifted with the ability to see countless ways of inviting others into a fresh encounter with Jesus, and are busy at work matching the context and its needs with new expressions and methods.

These guides are often seen by the existing church establishment as risky, and even dangerous, and kept at arm's length. But once their heart is revealed, we see a deep passion for the life Jesus lived. They are unapologetic for their pursuit of a people and a church that looks more like him, calling us out of our unbelief, and inviting us to take the next step in following Jesus. Spiritual Entrepreneurs exhibit an early-adopter mentality.

They act first and worry about all the details much later (Matthew 14:29; John 21:7). They are not theorists, but rather practitioners. They are part Peter who instinctually went first, and part Paul who was passionate to reach further. They also are part Joshua, who took on leading the people of God into the unknown, and to places where they had never been.

SPIRITUAL ENTREPRENEURS OFTEN FACE THESE TWO CHALLENGES:

1) Many fear entrepreneurs and therefore withhold their trust. As is true of most who exhibit prophetic insights/gifting, the truth they demonstrate is resisted and many are reluctant to follow. Some even fear them because of the abuse that has occurred at the hands of those focused on personal ambition, as opposed to Kingdom initiatives.

2) Entrepreneurs live in the minority, both within the general population, and within a risk-averse church. It is estimated that, in total, entrepreneurs are only 16% of the American workforce.[2] I suspect that an even lower percentage resides in today's church. It is difficult for Spiritual Entrepreneurs to serve and work with those who share their belief in Christ, and yet live in such practical unbelief, resulting in many such entrepreneurs taking their gifts outside the walls of the church.

IDENTIFYING SPIRITUAL ENTREPRENEURS

In the days ahead, nomads will need the insights, language, and new expressions that Spiritual Entrepreneurs provide. Without these guides ahead of us, many will become discouraged and will leave the nomadic journey.

HERE ARE SEVERAL WAYS TO BETTER RECOGNIZE SPIRITUAL ENTREPRENEURS:

- They ask the questions of "Why?" that the rest of us leave unspoken and speak to the doubts and fears each of us possess when considering something new.
- They are self-defined and do not require the full agreement or approval of others in order to move forward.
- They have a passion to see others join the creative process and invite them to offer their unique gifting.
- They are quick to trust and include others who desire to join new ventures, sometimes to their own detriment.
- They have an ability to translate, communicate, and promote new norms that can help counteract the fears that easily hold back the new expression being formed.

MEET HUGH HALTER

Hugh Halter is a classic Spiritual Entrepreneur. He has guided hundreds of nomads and apprentices in their journey toward new expressions of church and missional ministry. For many years, his teaching and personal pursuit of a more authentic church have flipped the *paradigm* to focus on more Jesus apprentices as opposed to just more churches.

Hugh, along with his co-author Matt Smay, broke new ground in 2008 with their book, *The Tangible Kingdom: Creating Incarnational Community*. In it they introduced issues related to "missional community," and how faith is apprenticed in the context of life together. That book was the first of many that caused me to see the changes that lie ahead for the local church. I have appreciated Hugh's commitment to take along all those who have wanted to join him for the journey.

Hugh continues to push us beyond our current and familiar forms. He isn't bound by what we know or currently see as the norm. His eyes are on Scripture, and he hangs out on the edge of the church establishment, where he has seen Jesus do some of his greatest work.

In my view, while Hugh remains committed to new church planting, he has made the shift beyond the idea of just church planting, to multiple, new expressions of missional life. He has wed mission with discipleship, and sought to cultivate new environments where these, together, incubate a different kind of church.

Beyond just theorizing, Hugh is knee-deep in the work itself. He is pioneering community and city partnerships where he lives in Alton, Illinois. In 2018, Hugh founded Lantern Network and opened Post Commons with the purpose of "incubating good works." This community hub has become the living room of Alton and now serves as the innovation/enterprise/mission hub for those who serve in Lantern Network.

Hugh is a leading missional voice, authoring such books as *The Tangible Kingdom, AND: The Gathered and Scattered Church, Flesh,* and, most recently, the *Life as Mission Series*, which seeks to equip Christians to live the missionary life of Jesus in their everyday context. His newest endeavor comes with establishing the "Brave Cities" network, a collaborative space for nomads working to see the gospel in integrated forms of business development, justice works, and neighborhood transformation. You can learn more about Hugh at his website: hughhalter.com.

SOME OF HUGH'S OWN WORDS:

> *"The gospel is not about trying to wedge a little Jesus into our crazy lives. The gospel is about letting God bring redemption and the way of his crazy kingdom into our frantically dysfunctional patterns of living. Influence doesn't happen by extracting ourselves from the world for the sake of our values, but by bringing our values into the culture."*[3]

> *"We have to remember that the ancient faith communities that set a course to change the history of the world did so without church programs, without paid staff, without Web sites, and without brochures, blogs, or buildings. They were lean! The point of going without all the stuff is simple but profound. When you don't have all the 'stuff,' you're left with a lot of time to spend with people."*[4]

NOMADIC REFLECTIONS

- Have you ever interacted with or worked alongside a Spiritual Entrepreneur? How would you describe your openness/receptivity to their approach and/or guiding?
- Are there any individuals in your area or network of relationships who could provide this type of "Spiritual Entrepreneur" help and guidance?
- What could an "outside-of-the-box" expression of church look like in your current context?

CHAPTER TWELVE

CURATORS OF THE TABLE

"We don't come to the table to fight or to defend. We don't come to prove or to conquer, to draw lines in the sand, or to stir up trouble. We come to the table because our hunger brings us there. We come with a need, with fragility, with an admission of our humanity. The table is the great equalizer, the level playing field many of us have been looking everywhere for."[1]

— SHAUNA NIEQUIST

WHEREVER THE ROADS AHEAD TAKE US...

We will find the table at the center, more so than the pulpit—conversations more so than convincing.

People are not objects to be converted, but unique acts of creation to be known. A meal is not to convince, but rather a place where life is exchanged.

THE TABLE WAS THE PLACE JESUS FREQUENTED, MORE THAN THE TEMPLE.

N.T. Wright states: "When Jesus himself wanted to explain to his disciples what his forthcoming death was all about, he didn't give them a set of ideas. He gave them a meal."[2]

In the days ahead, the table will play an important role in our expression of church. It is the one place where those we know, and those we do not know are both welcomed. Meals and lives shared around a table build bridges to new relationships.

At the table we sit, side-by-side, face-to-face, in physical proximity, where walls come down, and kinship is birthed. The distances and differences we often feel, or imagine, between ourselves and others, dissipate as we share in mutual openness and vulnerability. Curators of the Table help to facilitate all of this, and more.

PROFILE

Curators of the Table know how to *set the table* for others.

They create more than a meal. They curate safe spaces by utilizing their gift of hospitality, oftentimes around a meal, helping those present to discover common ground.

Curators of the Table know how to value *all* people. They create an environment where all have the potential to listen and learn from one another.

Curators of the Table offer authentic space where dialogue is organic, people instinctually find ways to connect, and there is a free-flow exchange of ideas. Here conversation is not contrived, but a natural byproduct of those gathered.

Curators of the Table author experiences, where those who come want to stay. To linger. To listen. To laugh. To explore. To belong.

THE TABLE IS NOT A NEW PLACE

For thousands of years, the table has been a place of *shalom*. A place where the cultural custom of offering a meal gives way to something beyond mere hospitality. We have lost touch with this rich and spiritual practice. These Curators of the Table are needed to reawaken our imaginations to practical ways of creating these transformative spaces. As meals are shared, as a glass of wine is savored, as coffees are sipped, the potential exists to experience conversation that taps into our desire to be known and awakens our innate need for meaning in this world. Where we feel the value of our personhood. Where we stop and listen. Where we come out of our isolation. Where we bring forth that which has been buried inside of us, into the open. Where, for the first time in a long time, we are able to explore the world of others. All because a meal has been prepared and set by a Curator of the Table. It is the vulnerability that comes from inviting someone *in* (to our homes and our lives) that offers honor and communicates care. This ancient custom brought forward creates the potential for new moments of transformation.

Curators of the Table are invaluable guides for the days ahead, especially as church congregations get smaller, focus more on community, and are located and operate outside of their buildings or campuses. As nomads transition out of the existing forms and spaces of the church, the table becomes a threshold and immediate new space that helps usher nomads along in their journey. This is the gift that Curators of the Table offer us. They facilitate invaluable space for nomads, creating times for dialogue and new learning around the table, counteracting the isolation and doubts that can easily arise as we journey toward something new. This way, Jesus' way.

There were endless hours spent around the table, as fishermen transformed into apprentices. Luke alone relates *ten accounts* of Jesus around the table with others. Things like a lavish meal being shared with a loan shark; an invitation to dine with the religious elite, interrupted by a desperate woman with a jar of perfume; and even quiet moments with just a few close friends, where feet were washed, and Kingdom values were put on display. *Extraordinary things happen around ordinary tables.*

As Jesus entered the homes of and shared tables with "outsiders," people like Zacchaeus, a despised tax collector, common ground was found where many doubted it could ever exist. Consider what this might look like in our day. A Christ-follower having a meal with a Muslim leader. A white, middle-class, Evangelical Christian, sitting down with an urban, city dweller who is African American. A conservative Christian accepting the invitation into the homes and lives of members of the LGBTQ+ community. A well-off suburban family, enjoying the generous hospitality of their immigrant neighbors, sharing in new food, drink, and customs. On and on. The table offers a place of acceptance, even when there may not be agreement. As Jesus was present at the table, the true nature and character of God was on full display: the love and acceptance of all. And though the religious leaders of his day scoffed, the outsiders and outcasts with whom Jesus dined, were moved by his openness. Curators of the Table provide us spaces where acceptance is found, love is encountered, Jesus is revealed, and nomads are changed.

THE GIFT OF HOSPITALITY

Curators of the Table influence others through the environments they create, and the kind of hospitality they offer. Most Curators will insist that they aren't doing anything special, just meeting needs they see, something any one of us can do. And yet their gift models the power of serving, and offers to each of us ways to extend hospitality to others.

"OFFER HOSPITALITY TO ONE ANOTHER WITHOUT GRUMBLING. EACH OF YOU SHOULD USE WHATEVER GIFT YOU HAVE RECEIVED TO SERVE OTHERS, AS FAITHFUL STEWARDS OF GOD'S GRACE IN ITS VARIOUS FORMS." —1 PETER 4:9–10

The practice of hospitality is about much more than just planning a nice dinner. It starts with cultivating a heart of hospitality. While it can be easier (for some of us) to entertain close friends or family, inviting those we do not know well into our homes and around our tables is where we truly learn the power of hospitality. The writer of Hebrews reminded those who were on the run, escaping persecution, being driven from their homes and places of belonging, to still practice hospitality. The strangers we choose to entertain may actually bring into our midst God's divine presence.

"DO NOT FORGET TO SHOW HOSPITALITY TO STRANGERS, FOR BY SO DOING SOME PEOPLE HAVE SHOWN HOSPITALITY TO ANGELS WITHOUT KNOWING IT."— HEBREWS 13:2

In the familiar story of Mary and Martha, Martha often is maligned because of her concerns over the needs of the meal, as opposed to choosing to focus on Christ alone. Jesus' exchange with Martha was not one of downplaying her gift of hospitality, but rather affirming a truth that all Curators of the Table know and believe that nothing is more important than time with Jesus. One of the great challenges of those who set the table for others is having the table set for them. Like any other apprentice, Curators of the Table can become so driven in their serving, that they themselves struggle to receive the care and hospitality of others.

MEET LAURIE YACKLEY

Laurie Yackley is a Curator of the Table. I'm continually amazed at how Laurie creates a table that is safe and welcoming, serving many from all walks of life across multiple cultures and over many decades. Though she shies away from the spotlight, whenever you enter a space or gather around a table that she has helped curate, the intentionality she brings and her care for each person she serves is self-evident.

Laurie seems to instinctively know what those who are gathered will need. She brings her tender heart to every part of the planning and preparation of a space or meal. There is a sense of complete acceptance that surrounds the tables she helps to create, inviting those all around her, especially other Jesus apprentices, to come, sit, stay, and join in the life and discussions being shared. Of all the things I've learned from watching Laurie and experiencing her hospitality firsthand, what strikes me most is the way she invites others into the moment and experience. Her ability to openly and genuinely communicate her desire to have you be a part of all that is occurring serves to disarm fear or apprehension, leaving each feeling welcomed, wanted, and valued. Every time you encounter Laurie, you will hear an invitation: "Come... we want to spend time with you... Come for dinner... Stay with us... Stay a while longer." Laurie models genuine care. Her gentle and non-threatening ways set you at ease. No one is left out. No one is marginalized or unwelcome. All are invited to join. Everyone has a place. Every person is wanted. No one is dismissed or passed over.

Laurie is also a Spiritual Director and, along with her husband Rob, Laurie's wise and gracious influence extends outward into our world through the ministry of Thresholds (further detailed in chapter 14). They themselves are nomads, who for the last thirty years have been cultivating new expressions of missional community and hospitality in a variety of neighborhoods around the world. And if you ever want the best waffles in San Diego, be sure to look Laurie up!

IDENTIFYING CURATORS OF THE TABLE

Here are three characteristics of those who can guide us in curating the table:

1) *Peace.* There's a genuine sense of purpose and contentment found within the Curators of the Table who are able to bring us together and create places of peace. They not only do the required tasks well (preparing meals, setting the environment, etc.), but they also recognize, acknowledge, and honor God's presence in each individual that they serve.

2) ***Authentic.*** Deep inside each curator isn't just a fascination with creating an incredible meal or beautiful environment. They see the Kingdom value of bringing people together,

serving them, and facilitating space for dialogue and discovery. Their great fulfillment is seeing genuine interest, laughter, mutuality, and hearts filled as new relationships begin to grow.

3) *Belonging.* Bringing people together is a call to belong—to participate in an intentional time of experiencing our common union. The time and space curated—to share a meal, to connect, to relax, and to join with others—is the catalyst and threshold to greater relationship and authentic community.

Tables are an essential element of the future church. To know one another not by our differences, but by the inherent value we each bring to one another, as unique individuals created in the image of God. The table is a simple and ordinary, yet powerful way, to become a different kind of church. The Curators of the Table will show us the way.

NOMADIC REFLECTIONS

LOOK FOR THE CURATORS OF THE TABLE IN YOUR LIFE CIRCLES.

Invite them into a conversation related to creating safe places of hospitality. Consider asking:

- What's important to them when they think of having a group over for a meal?
- How do they cultivate safety?

- How do they create spaces/conversation/tables where things feel natural, versus contrived?
- How do they know what people to put together, how do they then work to help facilitate conversation?

BETTER YET...

See if a Curator of the Table is open to come and create a meal, and/or time of conversation for your group, community, or tribe. Use this as an opportunity to learn from them, and further discuss how the table might be applied in your context.

CHAPTER THIRTEEN

MENTORS OF ENGAGEMENT

> "What is at stake is the credibility and promise of the Christian gospel, that we may heal the wounds of racial violence that continues to divide our churches and our society."[1]
>
> — JAMES H. CONE

WHEREVER THE ROADS AHEAD TAKE US...

We must face the racism and racial injustice that have, for far too long, been ignored, seeking healing, and empowering those whose voices have often been silenced.

The journey of a nomad is not a passive one. It is an intentional, active participation in the following of Jesus as he leads us into being a different church. It is a walk down the hidden back roads of the American landscape, engaging issues to which the local church in America has chosen to turn a blind eye.

Times of isolation always result in the loss of meaningful dialogue. When dialogue is lost, so is the potential for finding common ground. The COVID-19 pandemic exacerbated a growing polarization that already existed. The local church in America felt this reality again, most poignantly, in our inability to accept and address one of our deepest wounds; the racism and racial injustice found both in our past and present.

Racism and racial injustice are not just problems of America's past, but continue to seep into and affect the culture today. Rewriting educational curricula, blatant denials of past realities, or the naive response of Evangelicals related to the existence of racism in the church, does not change the facts, or its occurrence. The overt white supremacy of yesterday, and the white, Christian nationalist movement of our day have been comprised of many who claim the name of Christ. As hard as it is for many white Christians to admit, the local church in America *can no longer* deny its participation in this *national sin*. "In the 'lynching era,' between 1880 to 1940, white Christians lynched nearly 5,000 black men and women in a manner with obvious echoes of the Roman crucifixion of Jesus. Yet these 'Christians' did not see the irony or contradiction in their actions."[2]

Beyond those who are African American, Mexicans, Native Americans, Chinese and a host of other nationalities have also been subjected to the heinous display of hatred that is lynching, often carried out by the same men and women who had just come from Sunday services. Having been the perpetrators, and belonging to the *dominant culture* for so long, there is no way we who are *white* will ever understand these historical scabs that continue to be ripped open for people of color. The systems undergirding our American society have been skewed *white* for so long, that many of us are blind to see this reality around us. As Christians, we have no issue seeing the suffering of Jesus on the cross, yet we fail to even look at the lynching tree—a symbol of pain and suffering for so many of our brothers and sisters in Christ.

These are the facts that confront us today. The result of actual, past events. And once again, this is the crossroad at which we, as a nation, and we the church, find ourselves standing.

THE LYNCHING TREE HAS NOT GONE AWAY, IT ONLY LOOKS DIFFERENT.

From Emmet Till to George Floyd, and the many, many other men and women before, between, and since, all point to this deep wound and great evil still in our midst.

The existence of racism and ongoing racial prejudices within our society, and even our local churches, should no longer be an issue for debate. But the question each nomad must answer is, will they choose to inherit this problem, taking on the sins of the past, and begin the journey toward becoming a different kind of church?

Nehemiah chose to *inherit* a problem that was the direct result of the sins of his forefathers (Nehemiah 1-2). To inherit a problem is far different than just accepting that a problem exists, especially one of this magnitude. It requires the help of others, *Mentors of Engagement.*

While the other nomadic guides introduced are those who have journeyed ahead of us, and now call us to the new lands they have already discovered, Mentors of Engagement are fellow nomads who intentionally walk alongside. These guides are critical for us if we are to "inherit the problem," and address our places of blindness. We'll get more into that in a few pages, but let me first introduce you to two friends who have walked this road, together.

MEET HAROLD MCKENZIE & DAN NOLD

They are friends and each other's Mentor of Engagement.

For over thirty years, they walked the roads of State College, Pennsylvania, together. Dan Nold is white and grew up on a South Dakota farm. He has been the lead pastor of Calvary Church for 29 years. Harold McKenzie is black, grew up in Hattiesburg, Pennsylvania, and has been the pastor of Unity Church for 37 years. Both are married, raised their families in State College, and together participate in a regional pastor's collective.

Their friendship began in the early 1990s when Dan, who had just moved to the area, reached out to Harold, who had already been leading a congregation in the community. Though the two men came from very different backgrounds, over time they have built a foundation of friendship and trust. As they have walked together these many years, both would admit the road has been long and progress slower than anticipated. However, both would also agree they have gotten much farther together, than if they had made the journey alone. I asked them to share how journeying together has helped them take steps forward, both personally and with those they lead, in addressing the issue of racism in the church.

HAROLD SHARES...

I don't presume to speak for all black people. I don't presume even to speak for other peoples of color, because systemic racism in our country has impacted every ethnic group that is not white, from the Founding Fathers all the way down to this day. The challenge is that the church has let the world influence us. There's racism, bigotry, and bias in the church today. There are white brothers and sisters, who are not silent on these issues and are not indifferent. But when we look at the church as a whole, and its journey from slavery to now, we have had such a mixed record. And because of racism in the church, we have a racially defined church, and a demographic description of the church. We are the white church. We are the black church. We are the Hispanic church. We are the Chinese or the Asian church. But in my heart, and to my very core, I don't believe this has ever been the intent or heart of our Father. He sees us as his one church, one family. And so, it has become a passion of my heart these many years to see us come together, and fight this together.

DAN RESPONDED BY SAYING THAT...

Regarding America's racial challenge, I first go to my personal journey. My relationship with Harold has been part of that journey. I'll never forget one of the first times sitting down with Harold and Sherren (Harold's wife, a native of Mississippi), and she began sharing some of her stories of how racism impacted her as a little girl. As I listened, I just kept saying to myself, "This happened to a sister in Christ." Sometimes (when discussing racial strife) we get so caught up in the question of who did what wrong. But for me, at the heart of all of this is family. And that's part of the theme that Harold brought to me and taught me. I realized that I need to respond to this as a family issue, which for me, means responding out of a posture of surrender, vulnerability, and brokenness. It is me saying to someone like Harold, "I need you more than you need me." And, "You have been so wronged." I think God continues to try to teach me, and all of us, "You're not in control. You can't change the past." That causes me to feel vulnerable and produces a brokenness that becomes what I bring to the table. I bring not my ability to change anything, but my desperate dependency on God, to change me. That is all I can really bring.

HAROLD CONTINUED...

I hear lots of people who want to get back to normal [after the pandemic]. But for people of color "normal" is not a place we want to return to. This "normal" is what we've seen throughout history, but is now recorded on cell phones, and immediately sent all over the world. And so, this has created a deep cry within me, "This cannot go on." It is the same historic narrative, but played out in our era. Dan and I agree that God our Father is saying, "No! This is not about getting back to normal." The only way to see the changes needed is to make the choice to walk together, and not alone. As I learn from Dan, and he learns from me, that journey makes us different men, who can maybe influence others to live differently.

DAN REFLECTED THAT...

We (the white church) have a deep, deep desire for both comfort and control. Leaning in to these issues means giving up control, and moving right into the middle of uncomfortable. People will always choose to not engage the uncomfortable. And, if they believe that other people aren't as important as their comfort and preferences, they can allow themselves to think they somehow deserve the treatment they are getting. I agree with Harold, none of this will ever change unless I personally make the choice to walk with Harold, and Calvary (my church) continues the journey to walk with Unity (Harold's church). We must listen, learn, and lean into new behavior. I believe we are in a transitional season. A time when God is seeking to do transformational work in each of us. The goal is not to try to "return to normal," and move on as quickly as possible. The goal is to lean into this transitional time as much as we can, and allow God to do what he needs to do in each of our lives. God needs people who will surrender to his work.

PROFILE

Mentors for Engagement are those who step beyond mere rhetoric, beyond one-time events, and commit to the duration required for change. To them, engagement is first and foremost a personal choice. It is the same choice made by Harold and Dan. It is assuming responsibility for the problem and entering into the journey toward personal transformation. As nomads, Mentors for Engagement choose to inherit the problem, each and every day.

I WAS BORN IN 1952 IN LOUISVILLE, KENTUCKY.

From an early age, I was made aware of, and felt the tension of, racism and racial prejudice that surrounded me. My grandmother was a racist. Her anger and hatred for her new black neighbors resulted in her constant spewing of the "n-word" in my presence. The maddest I ever saw my father get was when his mother would erupt in this way. I remember a large, family gathering, organized by my grandmother, that included a distant relative who played an active role in the Ku Klux Klan in that part of Kentucky. He was a deacon in his church. Even as a young boy, I could sense the bigotry that lived just beneath the surface.

Our move to California in 1958, because of my dad's new aerospace job, placed us in the sprawling tract homes of the San Fernando Valley. A few years later, the race riots erupted in the Watts area of Los Angeles, bringing back those early memories, fears, and echoes of my grandmother's hatred. In my teen years, we moved a few hours south to Orange County, which landed us right in the middle of the labor struggles and racial tensions surrounding the Mexican farm workers movement, led by Cesar Chavez and Delores Huerta. My high school's "La Raza Club" led a student "walkout" in solidarity with the farm workers, many of whom were family members of my friends. I declined to participate.

And when I moved my own young family to Australia, I once again felt the tensions around race, as Australian nationals were confronted with a new influx of Asians to their cities. I remember attending a church board meeting in the role of a coach/consultant and hearing an elder declare: "Those Asians should just take all their money, and go home! We don't want them. We don't need them!" When I spoke up, I was met with a stern, "How would you know Yank? You are not from here!"

I am no stranger to the culture of racism in both its subtle, and overt forms. Throughout my life journey, it has reared its ugly head in the worlds that have surrounded me. Though I have witnessed its existence, and seen the harm it has caused others, I have admittedly turned a blind eye when it has occurred. Simply *acknowledging* its existence was not enough to cause me to *inherit* and face this national sin as my own. *How could this be?* Awareness of a problem does not automatically translate into the different behavior required to *inherit* it as a problem. To *inherit* a problem requires that a choice be made. One that involves a daily commitment to behave our way into a different future.

The James H. Cone quote at the beginning of this chapter speaks precisely to this reality, the credibility of the church is at stake. Will we make the choice to own our past, and change our beliefs and behavior? Founder and former President of *Sojourners* magazine, Jim Wallis, concurs with Cone when he states:

"IN THE END, WE CAN AND MUST SHED OURSELVES OF OUR RACIAL IDOLS AND DIVISIONS THAT HAVE BOUND AND SEPARATED US, AND FIND OUR DIGNITY TOGETHER AS THE CHILDREN OF GOD, ALL MADE IN THE IMAGE OF THE ONE WHO LOVES US ALL."[3]

INHERITING THE PROBLEM

Inheriting a problem means making the choice to see a problem as our problem, and taking personal ownership. It is identifying ourselves as guilty of the acts that have been carried out, even if we did not commit them. It means taking responsibility. It requires giving up our need to absolve ourselves, and others, of any wrongdoing. It is more than just confessing a wrong. It is taking on a posture of humility, allowing ourselves to feel the full weight of our sin, and mourn the deep wounds and destruction it has caused.

Nehemiah, the cupbearer to King Artaxerxes, took ownership of the devastation and destruction of Jerusalem. His first response was not to rally the troops, but to move into personal prayer, as he grieved and confessed:

"I CONFESS THE SINS WE ISRAELITES, INCLUDING MYSELF AND MY FATHER'S FAMILY, HAVE COMMITTED AGAINST YOU. WE HAVE ACTED VERY WICKEDLY TOWARD YOU. WE HAVE NOT OBEYED THE COMMANDS, DECREES AND LAWS YOU GAVE YOUR SERVANT MOSES." — NEHEMIAH 1:6,7

Nehemiah inherited the sins of his forefathers, as well as the destructive results of those sins, by walking amongst the ruins, allowing the full extent of the evils that had occurred to move him.

"I SET OUT DURING THE NIGHT WITH A FEW OTHERS. I HAD NOT TOLD ANYONE WHAT MY GOD HAD PUT IN MY HEART TO DO FOR JERUSALEM. THERE WERE NO MOUNTS WITH ME EXCEPT THE ONE I WAS RIDING ON. BY NIGHT I WENT OUT THROUGH THE VALLEY GATE TOWARD THE JACKAL WELL AND THE DUNG GATE, EXAMINING THE WALLS OF JERUSALEM, WHICH HAD BEEN BROKEN DOWN, AND ITS GATES, WHICH HAD BEEN DESTROYED BY FIRE." — NEHEMIAH 2:12,13

Inheriting a problem is an engagement of the sin that has occurred, and being courageous enough to see the consequences. In our case, this means seeing the generations of ruined lives, and the destruction that has come through centuries of hate, racism, prejudice, bigotry, and injustice. In one form or another, these are all still present in the *dark side* of American culture. The local church is no exception. The ownership that comes as we inherit a problem requires that we seek out those who have experienced these wrongs and injustices to walk alongside us in our blindness and serve as Mentors of Engagement. It is not until we *see it, hear it,* and *feel it,* with the help of a brother or sister, that the damage and destruction of this sin can become our own.

While I have chosen to focus on issues of racism and racial injustice, there are many other issues where the church in America has turned a blind eye. We have repeatedly seen the church become complicit as it has turned a blind eye to violence and war, to the horrendous acts perpetrated against native peoples, and in its exclusion and bigotry towards people of certain genders or sexual orientations. I fear history is repeating itself, as the church now turns a blind eye to the hurt and disenfranchisement experienced by the LGBTQ+ community.

THE CALL TO LISTEN

In my years of teaching others to coach, I have found the "Three Levels of Listening," documented in the book *Co-Active Listening* by Karen Kimsey-House, Henry Kimsey-House, and Laura Whitworth, to be incredibly helpful.

- *Level One listening* is listening primarily to yourself. In this level of listening, you are not hearing the other person. Mostly, you are listening to yourself, and your own opinions as opposed to what they are saying.

- *Level Two listening* is focused on what the other person is saying. You are listening to their words, seeking to understand, but interpreting the meaning of those words from your own perspective and experiences.
- *Level Three listening* is completely directed toward the other person. It is fully hearing and seeing what is being shared from their perspective—suspending all judgment or opinion. It is trying to see the world through the other's eyes.

Level One and Level Two listening can help us identify our need for change, and take steps to begin that process. However, Level Three Listening is where true transformation occurs as we see and experience the problem solely from the other's perspective, and not our own. It opens the door for the potential of long-term, authentic relationship.

A Mentor of Engagement offers a side-by-side relationship that differs from our typical model of mentoring where knowledge and skills are imparted by the "expert." This is *lateral, peer-to-peer mentoring*, built on a foundation of relationship and occurring over the long haul. In this case, it involves the exchange of knowledge, experiences, historical events, new skills, language, and paradigms in order to help one another see and understand from the other's perspective. It is the relationship we saw earlier, between Harold and Dan.

IDENTIFYING MENTORS OF ENGAGEMENT

I close with a partial list of some of the qualities and characteristics of those who could serve as valuable Mentors of Engagement:

- An apprentice of Jesus who demonstrated a commitment to personal growth and transparency.
- Personal vulnerability and openness, offering others grace and truth.
- Life experience in an area, people group, or struggle different from your own that you desire to understand.
- Lifelong learner who listens more than talks, and helps you process your thinking.
- Empathetic, humble, curious, and committed to a journey of support and challenge.

NOMADIC REFLECTIONS

THIS IS A CHAPTER THAT WILL TAKE TIME, AND AN INTENTIONAL STEP BACK INTO YOUR JOURNEY, BEFORE RUSHING ON.

- Consider for yourself questions similar to the ones below, to help you in your reflection:
- What am I hearing in this chapter? What is the voice of my culture, or upbringing, and what could be the voice of the Spirit?
- How have you chosen to respond to issues of race and racism in the past? What should be your response today? And into the future?
- Who could you travel with into the future, similar to the mentoring and engagement that Dan and Harold share?
- What do I choose not to turn a blind eye to in the future?

CHAPTER FOURTEEN

ARCHITECTS OF COMMUNITY

> "Christian community is like the Christian's sanctification. It is a gift of God which we cannot claim. Only God knows the real state of our fellowship, of our sanctification."[1]
>
> — DIETRICH BONHOEFFER

WHEREVER THE ROADS AHEAD TAKE US...

Authentic community, and the environments in which it occurs, are essential in shaping apprentices of Jesus. It was in community that Jesus discipled his disciples.

I live in Northern California, three hours from the Pacific Ocean's edge. A drive to the coast takes you over the unending hills and vineyards of Napa-Sonoma wine country, and through encounters with the mammoth Redwoods that dot this portion of the state. The Redwoods are one of California's greatest gifts to the U.S. landscape, worthy of many encounters. These prehistoric and majestic timbers have had the ability to survive all that has come their way. Wind. Fire. Rain. Storms. As well as those who have sought to profit from their removal. None have been able to thwart their survival. These magnificent giants provide an incredible lesson related to authentic community.

Redwood trees can grow to over 300 feet in height. And yet, one of the most incredible facts is that the roots of each tree grow only five to six feet into the ground. They are sustained because each tree's root system becomes intertwined with the roots of neighboring Redwood trees. This interweaving of roots is what gives these trees the ability to endure their many challenges and grow to incredible size. Each tree stands both alone and together, forming a resilient forest community.

Today's expression of the church frequently promises "community," typically in the form of potlucks, fellowships, and small groups. But only in rare instances does real, transformative community actually materialize. Architects of Community are nomadic guides who foster environments where the lives of Jesus' apprentices can be woven together. It is in these spaces that foundations for spiritual growth are deepened, and the resiliency needed to faithfully endure the many challenges we face is birthed. These guides are able to tap into the collective, shared passion for an authentic life in Christ, and foster a deep hunger for that to be lived out in community. They cultivate and nurture new spaces, practices, and sacred rhythms, where the one root system can grow, with each individual drawing upon the strength of the others.

PROFILE

Architects of Community are able to hold together at one time the many variables of community life and formation. They are able to address the need for authentic connection, the quest to apprentice the life of Jesus, and recognize the missional needs of a local neighborhood or city context. In addition, they know that when constructing a healthy community, the very environments or spaces in which these things occur are equally as important. Without new spaces and places of learning where restoration can occur, nomads will not make it in the days ahead.

Architects of Community create new rhythms, disciplines, and times of retreat where the practice of community becomes more than just attending a perpetual set of meetings. They are constantly shaping and reshaping how community can better occur. Above all, their goal is the integration of discipleship with mission. No longer do these two functions stand separate from one another. Instead, apprentices of Jesus are formed both in the intimate times of spiritual formation, as well as in external acts in the community. Therefore, discipleship becomes a eucharistic act as those in community break bread, partaking in the elements, as well as planting a garden for all in the neighborhood to glean. Sharing life together is the very heart of what it means to apprentice the life and ways of Jesus.

It was in community where Jesus formed his disciples, much more than one-on-one. And it was into a community that Jesus entrusted the future of his church. His choice of venue was organic, coming from the spontaneous sharing of his life, and it was relational, with the forms fostering the sharing of their lives with one another. His chosen venue to propagate this expression of new life could have been institutional, political, or systemic. Instead, Jesus chose the relational, walking out life together, to demonstrate and expand his Kingdom. The first disciples experienced personal transformation, and explosive growth in the context of life lived out together. The early church flourished as a result of its organic methodology. Gathering house-to-house provided an ideal setting for which community could thrive as "many were added daily" (Acts 2:47). Architects of Community see what occurred in the early pages of the book of Acts, and ask themselves, and the group, "*What if...?*"

Architects of Community are typically highly intuitive. Their sense and gifting helps them to recognize that which is at work helping to facilitate community, and what is holding it back. They are able to recognize, way before the others in the group, when spiritual formation has begun to plateau, and the group has begun drifting back to mere attending. They create experiences that challenge Jesus apprentices to live out of a deeper intimacy with Christ, and to courageously choose to take the next steps in their faith. They refuse to allow community to settle for what is easiest or most familiar. They know how and when to reach forward to new expressions and faith experiments, as well as reach back to the ancient practices that have sustained the church through its history. These guides are not afraid to wade into and interact with ideas or theological treatises that others consider off limits, or easily discount or discard based on their own church/denominational tradition. They are able to hold the truths offered in tension, even if they may not fully embrace all that an author or movement has to offer.

Architects of Community are focused on inviting others to experience and express the life and way of Jesus, and long ago took their eyes off of numbers and metrics. Instead, they have put their focus on deepening the group's intimacy with Christ and encouraging life together in neighborhoods or other shared contexts. For them, the size of the community is not measured merely by the breadth of its numbers, but also by the depth of their relationships with Christ, and intimacy with one another.

HOW ARCHITECTS DESIGN COMMUNITY

Architects of Community design the basis by which a community is drawn together typically using the following, important core components:

1) *Affinity* — Architects understand that they must identify, and often clarify the core reason a group of people come together. This gathering point may be shared values, or a common purpose or objective. More than just wanting to be together socially, these guides understand that healthy community is reflective of a shared commitment, and a covenantal purpose. Architects design the way this affinity can be expressed, and ensure its protection. For nomads, this is a call to gather around and commit to apprenticing the life of Christ with others, around a shared need or common context or commitment.

2) *Apprenticing* — Architects are designers of ways where apprenticing and reproducing the life of Jesus can occur. They incubate spaces and places where participants find authentic community, and their primary expression of church. Rather than the Sunday services, sermons, and

small groups found in current congregational expressions, these guides seek to facilitate the apprenticing of Jesus' life and way by developing spiritual rhythms, weekly practices, and other times of formation for the group. These guides create meaning and connectedness for nomads, that often surpasses much of what is experienced within the current local church format.

3) *Application* — Architects actively monitor and adapt the shared rhythms, practices, and activities of the community so as to more faithfully live out the lifestyle and mission of Christ. Too often, groups of believers, over time, descend to the lowest forms of obedience and accountability. These guides challenge nomads to move beyond simply gathering, and toward lives of greater integration and faithfulness to Jesus' way.

MEET ROB YACKLEY AND THRESHOLDS

Rob Yackley is the creator and director of Thresholds, a faith-based nonprofit that helps create and incubate new expressions of church, teams, and leaders that are capable of engaging a world that is very different from the one in which many of us grew up. Their name—"Thresholds"—is an apt descriptor of their focus to help passionate Christ-followers cross over from current expressions of church and into new ones. Thresholds is a team of creative practitioners who are each embedded in their neighborhood and who engage life and culture in community with others. They seek to live out their lives from a series of sacred rhythms, shared practices, and incarnational service. Their passion to inhabit their neighborhood provides a wide variety of opportunities to be a loving, healing, and reconciling presence where they have been placed. Rob and Laurie, (mentioned in chapter twelve), personally lead an intentional community of spiritual nomads in the Golden Hill neighborhood of San Diego, California.

Thresholds also serves as a catalyst for missional training and coaching leaders to cultivate new communities of faith and environments of discovery throughout North America and beyond. Groups like Thresholds offer glimpses into the future expression of the church, committed to offering life lived out together, woven into the lives of those they surround, and joined together in the celebration of the sacraments. As an Architect of Community, Rob's ability to design learning spaces and ongoing community experiences shapes the lives of Jesus' apprentices. As a thinker and strategist, Rob also works to integrate contemporary practices of personal growth with the historic practices of the Church.

In their book, *Thin Places; Six Postures for Creating and Practicing Missional Community*, Rob and co-author Jon Huckins document the six core postures of missional community: "In our missional community, we seek to offer radical invitations rather than radical hospitality. While our doors remain open to anyone in need of a bed or meal (hospitality that has historical roots in monastic orders), those who want to participate in our covenant community must accept the radical invitation of apprenticeship in the way of Jesus."[2] I highly recommend exploring the ongoing work of Thresholds.

MEET JON HUCKINS

As a part of Thresholds, and as co-creator of the Global Immersion project, Jon lives out his passion to cultivate personal, spiritual, and social reconciliation through participation in his neighborhood intentional community. He also architects learning experiences tied to peacemaking in places of significant conflict, both locally and around the globe. Following Jesus in the way of peace shapes his everyday life. He's discovered that peacemaking is an essential expression of the mission of God and is best expressed in community. Jon has walked alongside leaders from all over the world on streets of conflict within warring neighborhoods. Jon believes that the posture of peacemaking should be a central behavior of God's people, whether they reside in a war-torn part of the world or just on the block in their neighborhood. Jon is focused on engaging and supporting the growing post-evangelical community and their role in birthing new expressions of the church among the rising tide of spiritual nomads who are in search of a more authentic expression of the life of Christ.

Along with Jon's book written with Rob Yackley (*Thin Places*), I also recommend his book, *Mending the Divides: Creative Love in a Conflicted World*, written with his colleague Jer Swigart.

NOMADIC REFLECTIONS

- Who do you know that might fit this role of Architect of Community or that offers this kind of help to others?
- What are some of the new forms or expressions that you're considering as you think about joining together with other nomads? What challenges might you face in doing so?
- What help will you need to ensure that the forms of the future are not just a rework of the past?

CHAPTER FIFTEEN

COACHES OF THE SACRED

"For I know the plans I have for you," declares the Lord, "plans to prosper you and not to harm you, plans to give you hope and a future. Then you will call upon me and come and pray to me, and I will listen to you. You will seek me and find me when you seek me with all your heart. I will be found by you."

— JEREMIAH 29:11-14

WHEREVER THE ROADS AHEAD TAKE US...

Discovery will be key for nomads who must take personal responsibility for their own formation. We must move from the acquisition of more information to the living out of what we already know, resulting in a Christ-like transformation.

Whatever we are told, we often resist.
Whatever we discover, we are more likely to embrace.

Nomads are those who accept the challenge to turn *what they know* into *how they choose to live and behave.* They make intentional choices to listen instead of speak, ask before they solve, and seek to own a truth, before they proclaim it as essential for others. We live in the age of the practitioner. While new information will always be essential, what remains in short supply are those who behave according to what they believe, and whose lives have been transformed by what they know. While we can continue to preach sermons on "The Good Samaritan," what is needed most are those willing to walk as *Good Samaritans* in their unique context. The starting point of the nomadic journey is *personal transformation.* It is personal renewal that precedes and catalyzes corporate change.

Coaches of the Sacred facilitate conversations of discovery and obedience. Coaching becomes sacred when the conversations that occur move from concentrating on the problems we face, and onto the person whom God is seeking to shape.

PROFILE

Coaches of the Sacred offer nomads a trusted relationship in which to process how God is already at work. Some of the key characteristics of these guides are tied to the skills, abilities, and commitment to relationships that construct bridges of trust. The days ahead will be filled with new and challenging events and circumstances that will demand a need for those who can help us process all that is occurring. No matter who we are, or how long we have walked with Christ, you and I do not get to clarity alone.

Coaches of the Sacred recognize that the problems and obstacles a nomad faces are used by God to do a deeper work in their development. These guides walk alongside those on the nomadic path, helping to uncover the forming work of the potter, as he shapes our lives through new expressions of his love (Isaiah 64:8). Coaches of the Sacred assist nomads in deepening their walk with Christ, but also in encouraging them to *stay the course* as Jesus takes them into new lands.

DISCIPLING NEVER STOPS. IT IS A LIFELONG JOURNEY.

God uses the people, events, and circumstances in our lives as potter's tools to mold and shape us. Discipling requires a continuous series of paradigm shifts, and an ongoing commitment to move into new behaviors as apprentices of Jesus. It is imperative that nomads break free from seeing discipleship as a class to complete, a book to read, or a series of steps to take. Rather, discipleship is about rediscovering and recognizing the voice of the Shepherd. More than any other skill, Coaches of the Sacred help nomads gain greater voice recognition of the King.

"I HAVE MUCH MORE TO SAY TO YOU, MORE THAN YOU CAN NOW BEAR. BUT WHEN HE, THE SPIRIT OF TRUTH, COMES, HE WILL GUIDE YOU INTO ALL THE TRUTH. HE WILL NOT SPEAK ON HIS OWN; HE WILL SPEAK ONLY WHAT HE HEARS, AND HE WILL TELL YOU WHAT IS YET TO COME." — JOHN 16:12-13

Coaches of the Sacred also help promote an increased awareness of the Spirit's role in leading and guiding a nomad (John 16:33). Deep inside each of us is a collection of deposits (entrustments), placed by the Spirit. Coaches of the Sacred help draw out these deposits (Proverbs 20:5). They are the sum total, to date, of God's sovereign, shaping work in our life, which comes as the result of both positive and painful moments. These skilled coaches and guides help nomads take these deposits and experiences and turn them into core values and life convictions. This is especially crucial in the in-between times. God does some of his most important, shaping work during times of transition. It is here Coaches of the Sacred are essential in helping nomads clarify their core values and utilize them as keys to unlocking future decisions. (See Appendix for more on Transitions.)

As valuable as coaching is to the journey of those apprenticing the life of Christ, it can sometimes devolve into a coach offering their own solutions, projecting their own experiences or struggles onto others. This is known as "Shadow Coaching." In these instances, the coach is typically not coaching another, but rather themselves and their own issues. Because of this, it is vital that Coaches of the Sacred be those who coach from a place of health, maturity, and personal differentiation. The best coaches are, themselves, being coached by others.

In my many years of coaching and teaching others to coach, I have found it is necessary to distinguish between coaching and mentoring. In its most simple form, coaching helps draw insights out, and mentoring helps to place new insights within. Often, others use the term "coach" to refer to someone to whom they can go, to talk things through, glean advice, and obtain potential solutions. In actuality, this is a mentor. Whereas a mentor draws from their own wisdom and experience and tells you what to do, a true coach helps you unearth the truths and insights already within, so that you can chart a course onward.

I spent many of my earlier years playing competitive sports. Like with mentoring, the coaching found in the athletic world is again very different from that found with Coaches of the Sacred. Sports coaches are typically tellers, problem solvers, and decision-makers. They assess a situation and make the call related to the changes that must occur. In contrast, Coaches of the Sacred are primarily focused on drawing out insights that are already within by asking questions, synthesizing responses, and helping others make their own choices related to which way next. While attending university, I was confronted with my need for both a sports coach (baseball, in my case), and a Coach of the Sacred.

My university baseball coach, Carol Land, was a Christ-follower who lived his faith. He loved the sport we shared, but loved Jesus more. He saw coaching baseball at the collegiate level, as an entry point into shaping the personal development of young men like me. He went home to be with Christ in 2022, but in those early days of my journey with Christ, he helped shape both my love for the game of baseball, and more importantly, my decision to fully surrender my life and future to Christ.

Coach Land recruited me to play baseball and attend a Christian university. I was a pitcher, and playing professional baseball was my dream. Up until that point, my faith in Christ was really just the faith of my parents, and our family culture of regular church attendance. I had big plans for my life, so I left the church and "ministry" stuff to my sister who enjoyed it more than I. While I had some early success in my baseball exploits, halfway through my time at university, I unwittingly stumbled into a defining moment—this time off the field Looking back, it is easy to see how poorly it could have ended, both for my baseball aspiration, and more importantly, my walk with Christ.

It was the 1970s, and a culture of protest and defiance was all around. I took it upon myself to challenge the inconsistencies I saw from the school's administrators by leading a small, student protest. My questioning of those in authority at this denominationally sponsored school meant the loss of my campus job (half of my tuition), and put in jeopardy my baseball scholarship (the other half). I was at a crossroads.

I will never forget the day Coach Land called me to his office and told me that he could see what was happening. I was being scapegoated, and made an example of, because I wasn't playing the church-and-school-politics game. At that moment, he became much more than a baseball coach. He became a coach of the sacred work God was doing in my life. He asked me what I wanted out of life. He listened. He drew out my latent desire to see my life count for Christ. He helped walk me through, by walking alongside. Coach Land helped me see how God was at work in my life, even in a moment of great confusion and disappointment. He also turned his belief in me into a continuing scholarship. What could have become a moment that drove me away from Christ, instead became a sacred moment in which I surrendered to Christ, and the next chapter in my discipleship. Though I never became the baseball player that he and I dreamed I could be, I experienced the power of real coaching. I saw how breakthrough moments can occur when someone comes alongside and helps us process the challenging moments in life. It was one of the reasons I decided to become a Coach of the Sacred.

In some ways, Coaches of the Sacred serve a role similar to that of spiritual directors. The difference is that these guides offer a wide-angle approach in processing one's lifelong, personal development, as opposed to primarily focusing on issues of spiritual formation like spiritual directors. Coaches of the Sacred help apprentices of Jesus to hear his voice and obey, over the long haul, as well as to process what God might be revealing regarding their future direction.

One final nuance that distinguishes Coaches of the Sacred is that while they primarily assume a coaching posture, they may also incorporate periodic moments of mentoring when it's needed. Their first call and focus is to draw out that which God is at work doing in an individual's life. They do this by creating a relational bridge of trust. But at times in that relationship, those they coach need input and new paradigms to help them process all that is occurring. Blind spots can occur as each of us journey and grow. Feedback is needed to point out that which goes unseen, or even unknown. In those moments, Coaches of the Sacred are skilled at placing new insights within, while being certain to return to their role as coach, and helping those they coach process their next steps.

Nomadic guides who serve as Coaches of the Sacred are able to bring together these three, essential skills as they help others:

1) The skill of drawing out how God is at work (coaching).
2) The skill of listening to the Holy Spirit, who continues to lead and guide us into all truth.
3) The skill of identifying issues of formation and the lifelong development of Christ-followers.

REMEMBERING PAUL RHOADS

My friend Paul Rhoads left us suddenly in 2019, far too early.

Without a doubt, Paul was the epitome of one who was a Coach of the Sacred.

Paul possessed an incredible blend of a deep passion for spiritual formation, and a deep knowledge of the lifelong, leader development paradigm. We first met in seminary and later served together for 20 years within a missions organization. It was a time of partnership that left an undeniable stamp on both of our lives. Paul and I reversed roles, working for each other several times, but it was our commitment to the local church and the shaping of the lives of leaders that yielded his greatest deposits in my life, and in the lives of hundreds.

Paul and I instinctually knew that coaching was ministry, more than just problem solving, and that God brings many into coaching to do a deeper work within them. At times, we used a tag-team approach, Paul would speak into the lives of leaders related to their spiritual formation, as I would come alongside and help them clarify their unique contribution. He taught me to see our times of coaching others as an opportunity to help them join in the Triune dance occurring within the communion of the Father, the Son, and the Holy Spirit. In the end, he joined and worked with SoulFormation, an academy for spiritual formation, where he focused on training spiritual directors. He was a unique blend of coach and spiritual director, and impacted each of our lives with a greater capacity to see how Jesus was at work in our lives, using the very life experiences we encountered, to shape us.

AS I THINK OF WHAT PAUL TAUGHT ME ABOUT COACHING THE SACRED, A SIMPLIFIED SUMMARY WOULD INCLUDE THE FOLLOWING:

- They listen between the words.
- They ask questions beyond the obvious.
- They look for doors that open up someone's interior life.
- They call out deeper longings.
- They unearth an existing hunger for God, unknown to the one they coach.
- They help others to see that they often don't live out of their "true self."
- They challenge others to desire and grow in their self-awareness.
- They call those they coach to lead out of a place of greater health.
- They center their lives around apprenticing the life and way of Jesus.

In writing this, I am once again reminded how much I miss Paul. He did for me, and for so many others, that which each nomad will need as they walk out this journey, namely someone committed to their personhood and growth. Though few will equal Paul's passion and skill, may his tribe increase to help the nomads of today stay the course, into the future.

Leader Breakthru (my organization) has trained hundreds to be Coaches of the Sacred. Each one of those we recommend has been trained to coach the person, instead of just the problem, utilizing the IDEA Coaching Pathway, and personal development resources developed over the last decades.

Our coaches are equipped to help nomads discern the leading of the Holy Spirit and chart their next steps forward. You can learn more about the IDEA Coaching Pathway, find a coach to walk with you, and explore our many resources related to lifelong development on our website, leaderbreakthru.com.

NOMADIC REFLECTIONS

- How do these thoughts on sacred coaching change or enhance your view of coaching?
- Who do you know, or where could you turn, to find this type of help or guidance as you journey into the future?
- Who serves as a Coach of the Sacred for your community, tribe, or group? What are the characteristics of the guide that you think your community might need?

CHAPTER SIXTEEN

CONVENERS OF RELATIONSHIPS

"He answered… 'Love the Lord your God with all your heart and with all your soul and with all your strength and with all your mind'; and, 'Love your neighbor as yourself.' 'You have answered correctly,' Jesus replied. 'Do this and you will live."

— LUKE 10:27-28

WHEREVER THE ROADS AHEAD TAKE US…

Fewer and fewer of our neighbors will experience the transformative love and way of Jesus through Sunday-centric church experiences. Rather, they will encounter it through the life and relationship they share with their nomad neighbors.

In an age of unprecedented isolation, the world is in desperate need of good neighbors. Nomads are those who forge genuine, authentic relationships with the very people many church attenders drive past on their way to Sunday services... their neighbors.

Rosaria Butterfield has written a must-read book on the topic of loving our neighbors. Her story is one that captures the feelings and attitudes of those outside today's church, looking in. Writing in *The Gospel Comes with a House Key*, she states, "And here is the edge: Christians are called to live in the world but not live like the world. Christians are called to dine with sinners but not sin with sinners. But either way, when Christians throw their lot in with Jesus, we lose the rights to protect our own reputation."[1]

Conveners of Relationships are bridge builders. They have stepped over the line, and chosen to live out *both* of Jesus' statements as he answered the question: *What must we do to inherit eternal life?* (Luke 10: 25) As they have walked the roads of life, these guides have come to realize that the way they love the Lord their God is by loving their neighbor next door.

Conveners of Relationships love their neighbors, not with the motive to change their neighbors, but rather in acknowledgment that they need their neighbors more than their neighbors need them. God uses these relationships and the circumstances that transpire, as a way to reveal the character of his love, for each of us. The choice to leave our world, and enter the world of another, is the road by which nomads apprentice the life of Jesus (Mark 12:30-31).

BEFORE WE GO ANY FURTHER...

There is an important misunderstanding from the Church Growth era that must be fully discarded. The call to love our neighbors is not a command to be lived out in order to manipulate people to attend church. Loving our neighbors is not an outreach program or tied to growing the church. Our only motive must be to love our God. As my good friend Rob Yackley has taught me, when we love our neighbors through tangible acts and interactions, we must put aside our agenda for conversion or church attendance, while not letting go of the hope that Christ would encounter them.

There! I feel better. Let's continue.

PROFILE

Conveners of Relationships have the capacity and have learned ways to engage in relationship. They connect to the lives of those who live next door, but also with work associates, extended family members, young people, old people, sinners, saints, anyone and everyone with whom they share the world: their neighbors. They do not see individuals as projects or mission targets to be reached but as people, like themselves, searching for purpose and belonging.

Conveners of Relationships see behind the veneers and masks that many of us wear. To these guides, people deserve to be known *for who they are*, as opposed to who the world, the culture, or life's circumstances have forced them to be. They see others as image bearers of the Creator, and value them accordingly. Whilc cach individual rclationship and journcy takcs on a unique form, these bridge builders hold as sacred the call to love our neighbor as ourselves.

While living in Australia, I learned of the Cape St George Lighthouse, which was constructed in 1860. The lighthouse was built near Jervis Bay Village, near the entrance to Jervis

Bay. It was to be a guide for ships returning to the mainland from the Tasmanian Sea. But there was a problem with this lighthouse. Construction began in 1856 without first securing the proper permissions from the Pilots Board, the governing authority. Numerous complaints poured in as construction got underway, mostly related to the location of the lighthouse. It turns out that it was actually built miles from where the builder originally intended. An investigation by the authorities found that the map used to determine the site had somehow been drawn incorrectly. And yet, despite all the controversy, the lighthouse construction was allowed to continue, and the beacon light was installed, and made operational. It was commissioned on October 1, 1860.

The problem with the lighthouse location soon became incredibly clear. The beacon light could not be seen from the ships as they were approaching the harbor, neither from the north nor the south. When the Pilot Board looked into the problem, they discovered that the lighthouse had been built nearer to the stone quarry for the sake of convenience even though it was 2.5 miles from the original intended location.

Astonishingly, the lighthouse remained in operation for nearly 30 years. Spanning the years 1864 to 1893 there were 23 shipwrecks and with them, the corresponding loss of life. Finally, the lighthouse was decommissioned. It was replaced by Point Perpendicular Lighthouse in 1899. The new lighthouse was positioned in a place where ships were better able to see its light and receive help navigating the dangerous cape.

For all those many years, the original lighthouse along the cliffs of Cape St George had misled captain after captain and caused shipwreck after shipwreck. Something that was so needed, by so many, and existed for so many years, was in a place where so few would ever see its light, and the hope it offered.[2]

I am still baffled by the church attenders who wonder why their neighbors refuse to come to church, or want little to do with church people. It is the narrative we just read. It's about lighthouses that have failed to shine their light where it was needed, which has resulted in the shipwrecked lives that exist all around us. We must come to terms with the reality that for decade after decade, the light that the church has to offer to guide the lost home, has been misplaced, like the original Cape St George lighthouse, locked within the four walls of the church. If the light of Christ, is to be seen in the darkness, it must be placed right where it is needed the most: alongside the lives of our neighbors.

YOU CANNOT LOVE YOUR NEIGHBOR, IF YOU ARE NEVER IN THE NEIGHBORHOOD.

Whether that be a literal neighborhood made up of homes or apartments, a workplace, a pub, or coffee shop, or even a park, nomads understand that Jesus brought light to the very places where he and his neighbors lived their lives. This looked like discussions right out in the streets of his village/neighborhood of Capernaum and continuing over a meal at Peter's house. The life of Jesus was not centered around the synagogue or tied to the temple. It was an organic, natural extension of the flow of life already occurring around him. As we move into the future, the effectiveness of our mass outreach strategies will continue to wane. Nomads recognize this reality and choose to live out Jesus' way alongside their neighbors.

Conveners of Relationships are skilled at creating spaces where those who know Christ, and those who have yet to embrace him, are at home with each other. They build community around cookouts, block parties, wine tastings, s'mores night, coffee and donuts on the driveway, shared meals together, and so much more. These are spaces where nomads learn to shed the conditioning that comes with church life and evangelism methods, and simply be themselves. No agendas. No apologetics. No programs or prescribed talking points. Just you. This can be especially difficult for those of us who have been in vocational ministry. Conveners are able to foster safe spaces where genuine dialogue can occur, and mutual trust can be formed. It is in this safety that conversations move past the superficial, and on to deeper issues like the heartache of a parent over their rebellious child, an abusive relationship, a lifelong struggle or personal insecurity, uncertainty around finances and making this month's rent, and much more.

I grew up in an Evangelical "brand" of Christianity that linked two words together: *agree* and *accept*. The formula was as follows: If someone's lifestyle and opinions did not "agree" with what the Bible said or what the church taught, then you could not fully "accept" them as a person. On the other hand, if you chose to "accept" an individual as a person, regardless of whether you shared common beliefs, values or lifestyles, then it implied (especially to other church goers) that you condoned those actions or beliefs, and you yourself might be headed down a slippery slope. While I would not describe my upbringing as legalistic or even fundamentalist, it was not far off.

This upbringing and early instruction created a battle inside of me. Do I really try his "love thy neighbor" thing with those who are obviously *outside* the church, or play it safe and not risk the questions and scorn of my church community? This was the discourse that continued inside of me, for many years. The real struggle came when I realized how much more I enjoyed being with those outside the purview of the church, especially because they tended to be more honest and real.

I attended ~~cemetery~~ seminary.

I have a doctorate degree in *Global Ministries*, and I have spoken to and trained church leaders around the world. Despite my degrees, I had a problem. I could no longer reconcile the words of Christ to "love my neighbor," with my Sunday ritual of driving past my neighbors on my way to church. It was my wife, Robin, whom I watched love our neighbors, and build relationships with those in our neighborhood, that was the tipping point. She collected their mail, reached out when she knew of their struggles, shared news of other's needs, and engaged in conversations and relationships. All the while, I kept reading books on how we must be a church that *loves our neighbors.*

That was when God brought me face to face with my hypocrisy. How could I continue to condemn and reject those whom I did not know? The agree–accept paradigm I grew up with was my familiar fallback answer. Finally, one day I could hear God (or my own guilty conscience) asking me a question: "Can't you just rake the leaves covering their front yard?" "No Lord, I don't want to!"

Really? I thought.

"Am I that hardened and entrenched in my principles that I can't even do a random act of kindness?"

Reluctantly, I waited until my neighbors were not home, and went over (in the rain) and raked the leaves on their front yard, many of which, admittedly came from my own oak tree! I finished, soaked to the bone. Freezing cold. And grumbling!

"There!" I yelled out loud! "I did it! Happy?"
No response from above.

The next day, our neighbor came over to our house.
I answered the door.

"Did you rake up all the leaves in our front yard?"
"Yes," I acknowledged.

"Wow! That was a lot of leaves! Thank you!"

"You are welcome," I responded, feeling validated and reaping my reward as a caring neighbor.

She continued, "But, I feel so bad. Our gardener is coming by this afternoon, and he would have done that! But thanks anyway. We appreciate it!"

That day I reluctantly raked their leaves, I never could have imagined all that would transpire, and the ways God would change me, as I shared life with them. From looking after each other's places when we're out of town, to sharing the bounty of our respective vegetable gardens or fruit trees, to spending afternoons with the husband as he was dying of Lou Gehrig's disease, and walking with his widow in her subsequent season of grief, God has resurrected me into a new and more full life. And all along I have needed them, more than they have needed me.

IDENTIFYING CONVENERS OF RELATIONSHIPS

Conveners of Relationships are all around us. Their life and lifestyle move *towards* the people God brings into their path, and invites them into authentic relationship. For these guides, loving their neighbors is not a project or event to be forced into an already busy schedule. It is simply how they do life. You can recognize Conveners of Relationships by the steady stream of stories they share of those they are connecting with and meeting.

Here are some qualities and characteristics to look for as you seek to identify and learn from these valuable guides. Conveners of Relationships are:

- *Gatherers.* They look for and find ways to bring people together. They take risks and try out ideas that others say will never work.
- *Includers.* They see and minister to those who feel isolated and shut out. They find ways to include those others ignore or walk right past.
- *Connectors.* They work to connect others of like interest and passion in ways that are both comfortable, and simple. They create a sense of safety as they invite others to move deeper in relationships.
- *Listeners.* They have practiced and mastered the art of good listening and are skilled in hearing between the lines and affirming the inherent value of others.

MEET JONATHAN WIEBEL

I've never met someone quite like Jonathan Wiebel. He has become both a friend and a guide to me, teaching me how investing time in relationships offers new life to both who are involved. He is a Convener of Relationships if ever there was one! But it hasn't always been so. He comes from the worlds of rock-n-roll and church planting, and has a heart to see the church be much more authentic. He and his wife Suzy are part of a growing number of Jesus' apprentices with whom I continue to intersect. They increasingly feel more at home with those *outside the church*, than those inside. They are nomads who are choosing to intentionally build genuine relationships with all people— not just those who profess Christ.

Jonathan and Suzy's church is their front-yard, their dog-club, the musicians they hang out with, and anyone who comes around their fire pit to chat. More and more, they find comfort and friendship outside the walls of the church. This isn't because they dislike Christians, but because they have come to see *life and church as being one*. Each of their interests, passions, and hobbies have become possible connection points with their neighbors and have helped to create a sense of *church* in the neighborhood.

Through two decades of youth ministry, church planting, and ruminating on Jesus' command to "love your neighbor," Jonathan moved full-time into Front Yard Mission in 2021. He now trains and coaches others to live out their apprenticeship of Jesus and love their neighbors in the places they live, work, and play. Along with his ministry partner, Steve Lutz, Jonathan has spent time helping congregations begin the journey of converting those that passively attend, into active Conveners of Relationships. Together they are working to shift the paradigm, so that we might see the front yard as the *place of the church*. This conversion process requires church attenders to learn the art of building relationships with their neighbors.

While this can be a slow process, it is vital for the church as we move into the future. As an experienced guide, Jonathan knows this, and has learned that when churchgoers start to see their front yard as a place to apprentice the life of Jesus, something powerful begins to occur. His passion is seeing nomads set free to help reshape this new expression of the church.

Jonathan summarizes the journey of loving our neighbors around four invitations:

1. INVITING PEOPLE INTO OUR SPACES.

We can show hospitality by inviting people into the physical spaces of our lives. It's sharing your front yard, back yard, home, and social gatherings with others. Inviting the people around you to join you around the fire pit, the kitchen table, or a family party can have far-reaching impact. Hospitality is actually a biblical value that believers are repeatedly commanded to embody.

2. INVITING PEOPLE INTO OUR LIVES.

Once people enter into our spaces, we can invite them into the potential of deeper relationship. As you lead with vulnerability, letting people see and hear your story, you open doors for others to become known as well. Jesus led with vulnerability when he asked the woman at the well for some water (John 4). Reaching out to your neighbors is not a project, nor does it make them a "target." Instead, it's a relationship that often starts with a need. And sometimes, it could mean you needing them.

3. INVITING PEOPLE INTO THE LIFESTYLE OF JESUS.

As you share more of your life with others, more and more of what you share will begin to touch on your reasons—that is, the *whys* of your life. Invitations on this level often includes informal events, like a meal together, sharing activities around holidays, and even enjoying times with friends who are other believers. The church is people, so bringing people into relationship with other believers brings them into the life and love of Jesus.

4. INVITING PEOPLE INTO A JOURNEY WITH JESUS.

People must first see Jesus before they can consider following Jesus. But they also can't believe in a gospel that they haven't heard. In the words of Paul: "And how can they believe in the one of whom they have not heard…? How beautiful are the feet of those who bring good news" (Romans 10:14-15). The invitation for someone to also join in apprenticing the life of Jesus is often the result of first seeing his life and way incarnated in the front yard. Learn more about Jonathan and Front Yard Mission at his website: frontyardmission.com.

NOMADIC REFLECTIONS

- How would you describe your current posture and engagement with your neighbors/neighborhood?
- Who around you has already built relational bridges in your neighborhood or another "front yard" (for example, your work place)? Could they be your guide and coach?
- What challenges do you personally foresee when it comes to moving your expression of church out into the front yard? What might be a first step?

CHAPTER SEVENTEEN

THE FIVE-FOLD LEADERS

The new church that is emerging is a radical reset of what it means to be the church. It is a return to the command to make disciples—apprentices who are passionate to live out the life and way of Jesus. It is a move out of the institutional expressions we have sought to sustain for so long, and into the streets and neighborhoods. It is reestablishing the function of the church as preeminent, as opposed to just its past, familiar forms. It is entrusting the church and its future, into the hands and hearts of those whose lives are patterned after the Kingdom values of Christ.

When considering the future form of the church, inevitably, questions of organization, oversight, and accountability will be asked. *"Who will oversee all this? What will keep these new expressions of the church in check?"* Questions like these are vestiges of our deeply ingrained, institutional habits, and our desire to organize and bring new expressions back under our control. Wendell Berry said it best through the beloved barber of the fictional town of Port Williams, Jayber Crow:

> *As I have read the Gospels over the years, the belief has grown in me that Christ did not come to found an organized religion but came instead to found an unorganized one. He seems to have come to carry religion out of the temples into the fields and sheep pastures, onto the roadsides and the banks of the rivers, into the houses of sinners and publicans, into the town and the wilderness, toward the membership of all that is here.*[1]

In his letter to the Ephesians, Paul introduced a five-fold approach to providing oversight for the Church as a whole. Each role is seen as a *gift* to the Church, offering an important function that contributes to the health and ongoing expansion of the Church. Many refer to this as the "Five-fold Leadership of the Church."

Alan Hirsch, in his book, *5Q: Reactivating the Original Intelligence and Capacity of the Body of Christ*, a book I highly recommend, has taken a fresh look at Paul's words, and provided an assessment when it comes to these five leadership roles in the church today. He states, "… the problem is that the Church for too long has only focused on teachers and shepherds at the exclusion of the others."[2]

Paul's words to the church in Ephesus reveal the gift of five types of leaders, given to the church at large, to help grow and mature the *whole* Body of Christ. They arrived on the scene to help guide the church forward, yet allow for its continued, organic expansion. The concept of the five-fold ministry comes from Ephesians 4:11. According to Paul, it was Jesus who gifted the church with individuals who would serve the unique role of apostles, prophets, evangelists, pastors, and teachers. Here's a short summation of each of the five-fold gifts of leadership.

APOSTLES

These are the leaders able to look ahead, focusing on the command that Christ gave to make disciples. Apostolic leaders are the groundbreakers and the ones who provide new, strategic direction for the church. They move the church beyond and are sent into places and spaces that the local church has often overlooked in the past. These leaders are skilled at weaving together mission and strategy. Whether the church exists in a neighborhood or has a regional or global vision, the help and counsel of these leaders is critical.

PROPHETS

These are the leaders who exhibit an intense passion and intimate knowledge of the heart of God. They possess an uncommon zeal for how that heart is to be expressed and honored in both our beliefs and our behaviors. They're able to spot when the nature and voice of God are being compromised, and when the church has drifted off course. Prophetic leaders are uniquely able to see how the Spirit is at work in the context of community, playing a vital role in calling the church to greater authenticity and faithfulness.

EVANGELISTS

These are the leaders who offer the church their passion to see the good news and truth of Jesus shared more openly within the places where the church has built relational equity. They want to see others encounter the love and power of Christ in transformative ways, resulting in more apprentices of Jesus. More than just proclaiming the Gospel, the evangelist keeps before us the mandate of the church to focus on reaching those outside its fold, and understanding its responsibility in "Jerusalem," "Judea," and beyond.

PASTORS

These are the leaders who care for the spiritual health and hearts of those who follow after Christ, tending to both individuals and the community. In the past, we've used this term to mean the "leader" (as well as "teacher" or "preacher") of a church. But truer to form would be seeing them as gifted individuals who provide holistic care. Pastoral leaders call for a continued and deepening pursuit of God and help us grow in our love and dependency on Christ. They lead us back to prayer, the Eucharist, and to loving one another within the community. They offer valuable help for tribes trying to better understand how to care for one another.

TEACHERS

These are the leaders who provide insight, depth, and application of the Word of God to the life of God's people. They are gifted at "breaking bread" and satiating the spiritual hunger of those who seek to know Christ in deeper ways. Teacher-preachers are able to provide fresh insights from the Bible, offering instruction that helps to align apprentices in both what they believe and how they behave. They provide orthodox instruction that keeps the church of today aligned with the church of the past.

Scripture is not definitive as it relates to *each* of these roles being present in every congregation or expression. I offer that each of these types of leaders be accessible, through a network of relationships, to help each expression as it seeks to grow and discern God's will. While all five are necessary and unique in the help they offer, it's possible that they may be individually called upon to play an important role at different moments in a church's lifecycle.

THE FORMS OF THE FUTURE OF THE CHURCH WILL VARY GREATLY. IT WILL NOT ALWAYS BE NEATLY ORGANIZED, NOR WILL IT OPERATE WITHOUT STRUGGLE.

In fact, I believe the days ahead will be marked by labor pains, as we give birth to and nurture these fledgling expressions. In addition to the unforeseen challenges that come with anything new, the church of tomorrow will surely face some of the same struggles as the church of today. It will be inherently imperfect, and susceptible to the flaws and ambition of people. I have often joked that the church would be a great thing, if it did not have people. In the days ahead, we must guard against our innate need to order and control, and instead allow the new expressions to be *unorganized*, able to grow organically around relationships, as opposed to recreating our old forms of institution.

Over time, I have come to believe that the Church was designed by Christ to be a grassroots movement. Its expansion was never meant to be controlled, but rather it was meant to be flexible, pliable, and contextual, able to adapt to the needs of those who are part of the community in which it finds itself. When the church has sought to become organized and managed, it has lost the elasticity required of new wineskins. We must do everything we can to allow for it to become, and then remain an organic and authentic expression of Jesus' way.

NOMADIC REFLECTIONS

IF POSSIBLE, BRING TOGETHER A GROUP OF FELLOW NOMADS ALSO ON THIS JOURNEY, AND PROCESS THESE THOUGHTS ON THE FIVE-FOLD LEADERSHIP:

- What stands out to each in the group related to a more *unorganized* approach to church in the future? What in this approach to leadership makes you feel hopeful and intrigued? What makes you fearful or uncertain?
- Which of the five-fold leaders do you imagine needing most in your respective groups or communities?
- How might those in your group, community, or tribe, who like or need more structure respond to this approach? How might their needs and concerns be heard and addressed?

PRACTICES

In *Section One*, we examined the call to live as nomads.

In *Section Two*, we explored new postures for the days ahead.

In *Section Three*, we surfaced guides who can help us stay the course.

IN THIS FINAL SECTION...

WE WILL TALK ABOUT PERSONAL PRACTICES THAT CAN HELP SUSTAIN THE JOURNEY OF NOMADS IN THE DAYS AHEAD.

In Chapter Eighteen... *Eyes on Him*
Taking our eyes off Sunday,
and fixing our eyes back on him.

In Chapter Nineteen... *Sacred Spaces*
Cultivating prayer and deeper communion.
Creating new spaces in our lives.

In Chapter Twenty... *Returning to the Mystery*
Releasing our need to be in control,
and letting the mystery return.

In Chapter Twenty-one... *Hope from the First Fruits*
A beginning look at the new that is emerging.

CHAPTER EIGHTEEN

EYES FIXED ON HIM

Taking our eyes off Sunday.
Placing our eyes back on him.
Loving God for God's sake.

"IT BECOMES HARD TO REALIZE THAT THE FOUNDATIONS OF THE ORDER OF THINGS, AS YOU KNOW IT, MAY HAVE CEASED TO EXIST. OUR GENERAL ASSUMPTION IS THAT THE ENVIRONMENT IN WHICH WE LIVE WILL ESSENTIALLY REMAIN THE SAME. THIS LEADS TO FALSE SECURITY IN WHICH WE CAN PRESUME THINGS WILL REMAIN THE SAME, AND PRESUME THAT TRUE DEPENDENCE ON GOD IS OPTIONAL."[1] — MARK SAYERS

IN THE "DID YOU KNOW" CATEGORY...

Many reading this book will already know that the Greek word for church is *ekklesia*. And, you may also know that ekklesia joins together a preposition "ek" (meaning "out of") and a verb "kaleo" (meaning "to call"), giving ekklesia the literal meaning of "the called-out ones." The apostles used the word ekklesia over 100 times in describing who they were as followers of Jesus, and ekklesia was the favored term of Paul when he dispatched his various letters to believers scattered throughout Asia Minor. What may not be known is that in 1525, one of the first to translate the Bible into English, William Tyndale found he could not translate *ekklesia* directly into English, and settled for the word "congregation." Then in 1611, the decision was made by the King James Bible translators to permanently drop the consideration being given to the translation of the word ekklesia as "called-out ones," and adopt the word "church" or "congregation" instead. Since that time, most English translations have followed suit, utilizing the words: *assembly, congregation*, or *church* in its place.

The contrast between "to call out" in English, and "to assemble" or "congregate," conveys two very different, descriptive summations of what it means to be the church. It is a shift from action, and the call to live out lives of worship *(verb... to call out)*, to that of gathering together in a place and becoming those who faithfully attend worship services *(noun... congregation or assembly)*.

MY POINT:

We have lost something of great importance in the translation.

It is clarified in this summation of the moment of Christ's death... "The God who made the world and everything in it is the Lord of heaven and earth and does not live in temples built by human hands" (Acts 17:24).

God moved out of the building.

Jesus' mission and message was not about filling the synagogues, the Temple, or our church buildings of today. Rather he came to fill a people who were "called out," and whose very lives have now become the temple in which he dwells (1 Corinthians 6:19,20).

READ WITH ME ... ONE MORE TIME:

"The God who made the world and everything in it … does not live in temples built by human hands."

Jesus' death and resurrection signaled something completely new… something far different than the religious order and structures of his day. He pointed then, and today, to lives lived differently, called out. A people who lived lives of worship, as opposed to more places of worship.

- No longer was worship to be about a place made by human hands.
- No longer was worship performed as a system of rituals, forms, and acts of worship.
- No longer was there a place or a human being who stands between us and God's holy presence.
- No longer would a temple, institution, or organized religion be required to gain access to God.

"THEREFORE, SINCE WE ARE SURROUNDED BY SUCH A GREAT CLOUD OF WITNESSES, LET US THROW OFF EVERYTHING THAT HINDERS AND THE SIN THAT SO EASILY ENTANGLES. AND LET US RUN WITH PERSEVERANCE THE RACE MARKED OUT FOR US, FIXING OUR EYES ON JESUS, THE PIONEER AND PERFECTER OF FAITH." — HEBREWS 12:1-2

IT HAS ALWAYS BEEN HARD FOR THE PEOPLE OF GOD TO TAKE THEIR EYES OFF OF PLACE.

It has often been even harder to keep their eyes fixed on Jesus alone. In fact, I would suggest that a core battlefront for the church, down through the decades, has not been the influence of the culture, but our misplaced attention and affection. From a tower constructed at Babel, to a Temple built by Solomon, to the Cathedrals of Europe to the mega-churches of America. We who say that we love God, have always drifted away from our focus on living out the life of Jesus, and become enamored by the places, and the things, built by human hands. David's cry out to God seems to recognize this dilemma we often create for ourselves. "You do not delight in sacrifice, or I would bring it; you do not take pleasure in burnt offerings. My sacrifice, O God, is a broken spirit; a broken and contrite heart you, God, will not despise" (Psalm 51:16,17).

Today ours is a Sunday-centric focus, with eyes fixed squarely back on place. We have once again constructed elaborate places of worship, while at the same time offering our world fewer and fewer who live lives of worship. To "go to church" translates into attending a Sunday worship service. I get it. Like many, I have lived out this focus on place for most of my life. I vividly remember the guilt I felt as a college student when it was time for the dreaded weekend phone call home, and having to answer the question from my parents: "Did you go to church today?" My answer of "no" felt as if I had betrayed Christ himself. It is why it was so ironic that during the months that surrounded the worldwide, COVID-19 pandemic, for the first time in my lifetime, and for many who were raised like I was, felt the impact of being told: "Don't go to church!"

For many, the pandemic became a defining moment. People stopped attending Sunday worship services, and many realized that (to their surprise) they felt closer to Christ. Lifeway Research has documented that: "Among those who now attend less often, half (49%) say a reason for this change is they found other ways to pursue their spiritual interests, with 21% citing [the pandemic] as a major reason."[2] That realization signaled to those who had held on for so long, that they were done. As they stepped back, they realized that they had changed. The local church of today no longer reflected who they were as a Christ-follower. The pandemic began to incubate something new; a lifting of the scales from our eyes and the launching of a deep hunger for a new type of local church expression in America. It is now a journey where thousands once again fix their eyes and attention, not on that which has been built by man, but rather on apprenticing the life and ways of Jesus, out in the open. For myself, that meant the challenge of letting go of all that had once been the focus of both my life and ministry. A task that was at times painful. I have often wondered if I had failed. Having focused my life efforts on seeking to renew leaders, and revitalize local churches, now Jesus was calling me to begin again. But all I ever really desired was to see more lives of authentic worship, with eyes fixed on him.

The nomadic journey is not a rebellion against church. Rather, it is a call for a major re-set of the local church. A refocusing of the people of God back on Christ, and to be those who "are called out," to apprentice the life and ways of Jesus. No longer could the new nomads live their lives under the banner and expression of today's local churches. As my friend Hugh Halter has proclaimed, these unlikely nomads are: "a new breed of ecclesial anarchists, who can never go back. None of us really are anarchists. We actually love the church so much we can't just let her mire in the mud of tradition and missiological missteps."[3] I applaud the appearance of the new generations that have now arrived on the scene, and who refuse to embrace the church they are inheriting. Theirs is a cry, coming from deep within the soul of the *ekklesia*, for a people who are willing to be part of a different, more authentic church. *Called out ones*, with eyes fixed on him.

I have had a wide variety of responses to the thoughts I have shared in this book. Some now question my commitment to the local church in America. Many of the comments can be summarized by the following questions.

- *Do you no longer believe in the local church?* I believe more today in the local church than at any time in my journey as a Christ-follower. I just no longer believe that today's expression of the church is viable for the future.
- *Aren't we commanded not to forsake the gathering together with other believers?* Absolutely we are to gather together (Hebrews 10:25), but that does not dictate the form or a requirement to attend today's local church expression.
- *Isn't it important to have a group of believers who provide accountability for your walk, and can speak into your life?* Absolutely. And while the local church is supposed to offer accountability, it rarely does so effectively. Most of the time, people have to go outside the church to find the level of accountability that is helpful and necessary for our spiritual formation.

- ***Don't you believe in the historical church, and the sharing of the Eucharist (communion) and baptism?*** I believe what I am describing is part of the historic church, and I believe in the priesthood of all believers. I also believe that some of the new, emerging expressions are actually closer to the church of the ancient past.
- ***Aren't we able to accomplish more together than apart?*** The church in unity is a mighty force for good. But it continues to fracture and polarize. I also see that the ability to effectuate change is now possible in a world that is knit together into a global community. I have watched humanitarian efforts often outstrip the church as people join together.
- ***Aren't we called to persevere, and remain committed to the local church?*** We are called to be the church, and faithfully live out the commands of Christ. Fewer and fewer churches are focused on apprenticing disciples, and lives lived like Jesus'. Ours is not a call to sustain the institution of the church, but to fulfill the mandate Jesus gave to his church.

One question I have been asked has revealed the depth of how the "institutional culture" has taken over the local church in America. I have been asked it many times, in different forms, but it goes something like this:

> *Let's say some of what you are saying could be right, Terry!*
>
> *If we were to shift our focus off of Sunday morning, and we let go of doing church like we always have; What do we do? Where do we go? What's next?*

Most feel lost without the survival of the institution. It is a flashback to the early days of the disciples. As Jesus began to reveal the real character of his message, many left and returned back to a religious system that they themselves despised. Peter's response was telling; "Simon Peter answered him, 'Lord, to whom shall we go? You have the words of eternal life. We have come to believe and to know that you are the Holy One of God'" (John 6:68–69).

The answer to the question above may sound simple, but it is the key to moving forward. *What do we do? Where do we go? What is next?*

We fix our eyes, once again, back onto Jesus.

We once again return to following the lead of Jesus.

We once again become his sheep,
and he once again becomes our Shepherd.

Back to that moment when something
originally called the *ekklesia* began.

Back to where all new movements must return.

To the beginning.

Back to our eyes fixed on Jesus, and not on place.

HOW DO WE PRACTICALLY DO THIS AS NOMADS?

There comes a moment in each of our journeys with Jesus, when we must decide that we will live out the rest of our days, in pursuit of him. Now is that moment.

Early on, God pursues us. But there comes a time when you and I must take on the role of the ones in pursuit of him. Duties, responsibilities, tasks, even serving in a church often become the very enemy of those who once sought to be faithful to Christ, and the church. You can only live lives of duty and responsibility for so long. The forsaking of the heart, and allowing the demands of others, to be our perpetual focus, is the recipe for burnout, and opens the door to religion. Our personal renewal, and a return to the pursuit of Jesus, involves a series of intentional choices related to once again fixing our eyes and attention back on Christ.

1) The choice of ***surrender***. It stands in direct opposition to our desire to be in control. It is all about our need to trust our King, as we seek him first and his Kingdom. The prize of surrender is the ability to once again see and recognize how God is at work (John 5:19-20).

2) The choice of ***alignment***. It confronts our need to lay down our preferences, plans, ideas and designs, no longer trying to negotiate what it means to follow Jesus. His ways and his thoughts are not ours (Isaiah 55:8-9). It is deciding (once again) that we must align with him.

3) The choice of ***brokenness***. It involves issues of dependency and the realization of our need for God, and a life of absolute reliance on him (Jeremiah 2:13).

4) The choice of ***vulnerability***. It is separating ourselves from reliance on our own abilities and skills. It is the call for transparency and living lives of integrity and honesty.

Making choices such as these begins the process of personal renewal, and a personal re-set of our lives, taking our eyes off of the things that have been propped up by man. Jesus told us the task of building the church was his, and he proclaimed that nothing would ever be able to overcome his work (Matthew 16:18).

For years, Richard J. Foster, and the ministry of Renovaré, have been calling us back to the practice of "fixing our eyes" back on Jesus. Foster has introduced many ways we can once again hear the voice of Christ, and have eyes to better recognize how he is at work. In the life of Bernard of Clairvaux, and his teaching on the "Four Degrees of Love," Foster, and others, have called back to the ancient Fathers, in order to move forward into the future.

Bernard of Clairvaux lived from 1090–1153. Having grown up in Dijon, France, Bernard went on to enter a monastery in Citeaux as a novice at the age of twenty-two. Just three years later in 1115, he was tasked with leading a small group of fellow monks to Clairvaux where he would found an abbey and remain for the rest of his days. It was here that the depth of his spiritual life would mature and transform him and those profoundly influenced by his life and teachings. Even centuries later, Bernard, widely considered one of the great leaders in spiritual formation, had a life-changing impact on both Martin Luther and John Calvin through the influence of his works. During Clairvaux's monastic life, he ministered to others, but he himself was deeply changed by the recognition of the "degrees" of love that can, and must, exist between us and our creator God. (The summary that follows is taken directly from Renovaré's article, "The Four Degrees of Love.")[4]

THE FIRST DEGREE OF LOVE: LOVE OF SELF FOR SELF'S SAKE

Love is a natural human affection. It comes from God. Hence the first and greatest commandment is, "Thou shalt love the

Lord thy God." But human nature is weak and therefore compelled to love itself and serve itself first. In the human realm people love themselves for their own sake.

THE SECOND DEGREE OF LOVE: LOVE OF GOD FOR SELF'S SAKE

God, therefore, who makes everything that is good, makes himself to be loved. He does it as follows: first, God blesses us with his protection.... Then, when we suffer some calamity, some storm in our lives, we turn to God and ask his help, calling upon him in times of trouble. This is how we who only love ourselves first begin to love God. We will begin to love God even if it is for our own sake.

THE THIRD DEGREE OF LOVE: LOVE OF GOD FOR GOD'S SAKE

But if trials and tribulations continue to come upon us, every time God brings us through, even if our hearts were made of stone, we will begin to be softened because of the grace of the Rescuer. Thus, we begin to love God not merely for our own sakes, but for himself.... Thus it happens that once God's sweetness has been tasted, it draws us to the pure love of God more than our needs compel us to love him.... The third degree of love is the love by which God is now loved for his very self.

THE FOURTH DEGREE OF LOVE: LOVE OF SELF FOR GOD'S SAKE

Such experiences are rare and come only for a moment. In a manner of speaking, we lose ourselves as though we did not exist, utterly unconscious of ourselves and emptied of ourselves.

If for even a moment we experience this kind of love, we will then know the pain of having to return to this world and its obligations as we are recalled from the state of contemplation. In turning back to ourselves we will feel as if we are suffering as we return into the mortal state in which we were called to live. But during those moments we will be of one mind with God, and our wills in one accord with God.

Eyes fixed on him involves making the transition where we begin the journey of loving God for God's sake, and not our own, the third level of love as described by Bernard. It is the pursuit of Jesus, for who he is, and not what he continues to do for us. It involves taking our eyes off of place and returning them back to who he is. Helen Howarth-Lemmel got it right when she penned the famous hymn: *Turn Your Eyes Upon Jesus*. It was inspired by a tract entitled 'Focused,' written by the missionary Isabella Lilias Trotter. The chorus must now become the anthem of each unlikely nomad:

> *Turn your eyes upon Jesus. Look full in his wonderful face. And the things of earth will grow strangely dim, in the light of his glory and grace.*

NOMAD REFLECTIONS

IF WE ARE GIVEN THE FREEDOM TO MOVE BEYOND A SUNDAY CENTRIC FAITH AND FOCUS, WHAT MIGHT THAT MEAN FOR YOU, AND THOSE OF YOUR TRIBE?

- What does it mean for you to shift the focus from seeing the church as one that gathers to becoming Christ-followers who are *called out?*
- How does a shift away from being a *Sunday-centric* church begin to impact your thinking and behavior in the days ahead?
- Who are the people with whom you would like to talk over the contents of this chapter? What core topics would you hope to discuss?

CHAPTER NINETEEN

SACRED SPACES

Sacred spaces are about holding your life open to the sacred.

Sacred spaces are about daily moments when we recognize God's presence.

Sacred spaces are also intentional times that are woven into the rhythms of our lives.

"THERE IS A GOD-SHAPED VACUUM IN THE HEART OF EACH MAN WHICH CANNOT BE SATISFIED BY ANY CREATED THING BUT ONLY BY GOD THE CREATOR, MADE KNOWN THROUGH JESUS CHRIST."[1] — BLAISE PASCAL

Viktor Frankl has suggested that between something being asked of us, and our response to that request, there is a *space*. A crevice in time. "In that space is our power to choose our response. In our response lies our growth and freedom."[2] Sacred space refers to crevices of time, found within each day, where we make the choice to recognize Christ's presence and experience growth. Though our lives may hunger for God's presence, he often arrives unnoticed unless we choose to hold space for the sacred.

Holding space refers to making the choice to reserve time, energy, and spiritual awareness of how Christ may be at work, using our day to shape our lives. It occurs in real-time, as we transact each day, as we are open and available for God to move and speak in the ordinary and the normal. When we hold space for the sacred, we are better able to recognize how God is at work using the events, circumstances and even the mundane as formation tools.

BROTHER LAWRENCE WAS A LAY MONK WHO LIVED FROM 1614–1691.

A casual observer of his life would have said that he lived a very obscure life, as someone who worked in a kitchen, doing the dishes, and preparing meals as one of the kitchen staff. But generations have come to know him as one of the great, devotional servants of the church, who created sacred space. Whether he was preparing a meal, scraping the pots and pans, or mopping the kitchen floors, he quietly practiced living in the presence of Jesus. Both leaders of the church and the common villager sought Lawrence for spiritual guidance and prayer. Brother Lawrence learned the power and impact of sacred space.

Brother Lawrence served in the kitchen of the monastery of the Carmelites, located in Paris, France He was given the job of cook and dishwasher for his community and although he thoroughly disliked his job, he embraced it wholeheartedly for thirty years. Normal, mundane days were often transformed into sacred moments as he recognized and welcomed God's presence. Lawrence believed in living a life in which every day, every thought and action he took, should be one with a focus on God's ongoing, shaping work. He summarized his perspective by saying: "I began to live as if there were no one save God and me in the world."[3]

The Practice of the Presence of God is a book that was compiled by others, documenting much of what Brother Lawrence practiced and believed, as he sought to cultivate sacred moments in each day. His thoughts included:

> *"The time of business does not with me differ from the time of prayer; and in the noise and clatter of my kitchen, while several persons are at the same time calling for different things, I possess God in as great tranquility as if I were upon my knees at the blessed sacrament."*[4]

> *"We should fix ourselves firmly in the presence of God by conversing all the time with Him ... we should feed our soul with a lofty conception of God and from that derive great joy in being his. We should put life in our faith. We should give ourselves utterly to God in pure abandonment, in temporal and spiritual matters alike, and find contentment in the doing of His will, whether he takes us through sufferings or consolations."*[5]

> *"I cannot imagine how religious persons can live satisfied without the practice of the presence of God. For my part, I keep myself retired with Him in the depth of the center of my soul as much as I can."*[6]

Our culture has so conditioned us to pack every day, every moment, and every space of our lives with the unending things that *must* be done. There is often no space for life itself. This is compounded in the lives of Christ-followers, who often feel that there is literally no time for God within their daily lives.

The life of Brother Lawrence can feel detached from reality. But the idea of *creating sacred space* is first, and foremost, a mindset before it is an issue of schedule. Sacred spaces have to do with how we approach and see the activities found within each day.

THERE IS A *SOUL-CRY* THAT CAN BE HEARD FROM THOSE WHO ARE TRAVELING AS NOMADS, HUNGERING FOR A DEEPER, SPIRITUAL FORMATION.

A longing for new ways and new paths that lead to a more intimate life with Christ. The way into that new place often begins by learning how to hold space for the sacred. Sacred spaces often become a threshold that helps nomads build a greater capacity to recognize and follow the voice of the Shepherd, as they walk on the daily path. Brother Lawrence provides an example, from his own words, that helps us better recognize how each moment in time can become a sacred space. Note some of the ways he approached the arrival of winter, and what this sacred space meant for his reflections on his spiritual journey:

> *In the winter I saw a tree stripped of its leaves and I knew that within a little time the leaves would be renewed, and that afterwards the flowers and the fruit would appear. From this I received a high view of the power and providence of God which has never since departed from my soul. The view I grasped that day set me completely loose from the world and kindled in me such a love for God that I cannot tell whether it has increased during the more than forty years since that time." He went on*

to say, "I have found that we can establish ourselves in a sense of the presence of God by continually talking with Him. It is simply a shameful thing to quit conversing with Him to think of trifles and foolish things. We should feed and nourish our souls with high notions of God which will yield great joy ...."[7]

BROTHER LAWRENCE'S REFLECTION REVEALS THAT:

- Spaces are moments of interior conversation.
- Spaces are about becoming true to who we are as spiritual people.
- Spaces seek to cultivate a deeper conversation with God.
- Spaces serve to grow our discernment, often yielding higher notions of God.
- Spaces reveal that which occurs that nourishes our souls.

Quiet moments. Short moments. Discerning moments. Open moments. Practicing the presence of God.

THE NOMADIC LIFE AHEAD WILL BE VERY DIFFERENT.

It will first be about the new work God wants to do within each nomad, even before we are able to recognize the form and texture of a new expression of local church. Identifying the sacred spaces in each day are first steps in recognizing the new work that Jesus is wanting to do in each of our lives. There are many correlations between the challenges ahead, and the unique journey of the first nomads, the disciples.

The first instruction given to these first apprentices that were *called out*, was telling. It spoke to their need to see their lives as a life focused on intimacy with Christ, even before they would understand their future influence for him. More than taking on a host of religious tasks, and the carrying out their roles as leaders in days ahead, Jesus set down the marker of life being lived out of the depth of their relationship with him. In the beginning, he highlighted that it would be easier to do, but more important to be.

"JESUS WENT UP ON A MOUNTAINSIDE AND CALLED TO HIM THOSE HE WANTED, AND THEY CAME TO HIM. HE APPOINTED TWELVE THAT *THEY MIGHT BE WITH HIM* AND THAT *HE MIGHT SEND THEM OUT* TO PREACH AND TO HAVE AUTHORITY TO DRIVE OUT DEMONS." — MARK 3:13-15 (EMPHASIS MINE)

The challenge of being ones who have been called out by Christ, will only be met from a base of authority far different than just our skills and abilities. We, like the early disciples, gained access to the authority of Jesus as we chose to live our lives in his presence. Each step, from that moment forward, was about being with him, and seeing each day from his perspective. Each day, every moment, practicing what it meant to live their lives in his presence, seeing and recognizing the sacred all around them. Cultivating sacred space for his new work within each of them. And out of their time with him, the authority to influence others to live out the life of his Kingdom (Mark 3:15).

From the very beginning, Jesus was forecasting to the early disciples (and us) that the most important thing a nomad can do is to cultivate the interior life with him. *Being* even before *doing*. Ahead is no easy journey. The journey of an unlikely nomad is not the same as a church attender. In so many ways, the life of a nomad will be like the fight of salmon as they seek to travel upstream. At other times, the life of a nomad will be that of a fish out of water. And with it, the inevitable questions:

- Did I really need to leave?
- Am I on the right road?
- Am I really part of the church if I am not attending church?
- Why can't I hear Christ's voice better?
- Am I really supposed to be doing this?
- What about all who don't agree with my journey?
- What are others like me feeling?
- Why not just let others figure all this out?
- Shouldn't I be doing something? Reading something? Taking some class?

NO LONGER CAN OUR INTIMACY WITH CHRIST BE RELEGATED TO THE SECOND-CHAIR of the Christ-follower's life, nor can we pass the responsibility of our spiritual nurture onto others. No longer can nomads hide behind the growth and journey of a great Bible teacher, insights from a trusted mentor, or rest only on the foundations laid by a family or local church. We each are called to be with him as we walk the journey ahead. This will require seeing him in the moments of each day, as well as becoming intentional in the cultivation of deeper intimacy with him.

MAKING SPACE

I was raised to have a "daily quiet time."

This was time set aside every morning to read my Bible and pray. It provided a great place to begin. But as time went by, I became restless. Wanting to move on to something more. I abandoned my daily quiet time, and I bounced back and forth between extended times with God, and stretches of very little time with God. Tension began to grow inside of me, mixed in with a little guilt. I decided that in the same way I sought to *create sacred space* in each day, I would seek to hold space for my own spiritual growth and intimacy with Christ, over the same time frames that I was using as I navigated my life: my week, my month, each quarter and the review of each year. I developed what I now call the *Every Strategy*.

THE EVERY STRATEGY CREATES A SERIES OF SACRED SPACES.

At first glance, this will look like another program. But its purpose is to help create new spiritual rhythms and spaces, each focused on establishing new ways to hear Jesus' voice. Each defined segment suggests various times to be set aside, but also varying spiritual practices to help cultivate a deeper journey with God.

- *Every day* ... space for God
- *Every week* ... space for solitude with God
- *Every month* ... space to engage in silence with God
- *Every quarter* ... space to search for the heart of God
- *Every year* ... space to consider next steps with God

EVERY DAY ... SPACE FOR GOD

30-45 minutes each day ... time of worship, alignment, feeding from the word, prayer and disciplined openness to what God is at work doing in that day. It can be helpful to have prayer book or devotional to guide this time. For example:

Common Prayer: A Liturgy for Ordinary Radicals—A daily liturgy and prayer guide.

The Blue Book Devotional—A great blend of Bible text and classic insights from the history of the church.[8]

EVERY WEEK ... SPACE FOR SOLITUDE WITH GOD

60-90 minutes ... an appointment time for you to disconnect and be alone. Time to journal, reflect, read, and cultivate quietness with God. Time to turn down all the conversation with others, and create space for you and God, to sit together, alone.

Use this time to journal about things related to your week. As weather permits, visit a favorite outdoor location. Time for a walk and conversational prayer with God. Time away from others. Time to be still. Not time to work. Time to just be.

EVERY MONTH ... SPACE TO ENGAGE IN SILENCE WITH GOD

4-6 hours (or a whole day away). Time to step back ... time to be quiet. Time to practice the discipline of silence. Time to listen vs. talk ... time to review your times with God ... to consolidate learning. An extended time to study/read/work on cultivating your life with God.

Here is a series of books that can help you think through ways to make sacred space.

Sacred Rhythms by Ruth Haley Barton—Ways to think about your spiritual journey, and times of silence.

Spiritual Disciplines Handbook by Adele Ahlberg Calhoun—Practical resource on how to practice and use the spiritual disciplines.

Divine Conspiracy by Dallas Willard—An Incredible read (and re-read) during this time. Calls you to go deeper into your journey with God.

EVERY QUARTER ... SPACE TO SEARCH FOR THE HEART OF GOD

An overnight away ... time for prayer and reflection. Time for reading, studying, and intentional personal growth. Time to review the year thus far. Time to re-establish rhythm and routines. Time to go after topics and dig deeper. Time to connect with a spiritual director or mentor.

Retreat centers and nearby monasteries offer rooms and meals for overnight guests. Some monasteries allow you to participate in their various practices. Check to see if there is a Benedictine monastery near you.

EVERY YEAR ... SPACE TO CONSIDER NEXT STEPS WITH GOD

A two-day, personal retreat ... away ... time to regain a big-picture view of your personal development, to reset the compass for the year ahead. First day—time to look back, where have you been. Second day—time to look forward. *Where are you going?*

Reflection Tool: Post-it Note Timeline—Available for free at leaderbreakthru.com/timeline

WHO YOU ARE BECOMING, IN THE END, IS THE MOST IMPORTANT THING ABOUT YOU.

"CREATION IS A STORY OF CONTINUAL NEW BEGINNINGS BECAUSE GOD IS IN A CONSTANT STATE OF CREATING … NOTHING IS EVER FINISHED."[9] — SHELLY MILLER

NOMAD REFLECTION

- What is surfacing inside of you when you read the idea of creating new spaces and intentionality in your formation?
- What will be your major challenges or obstacles?
- Where would you like to begin in becoming more intentional in creating sacred spaces?

CHAPTER TWENTY

RETURN OF THE MYSTERY

Christianity is a sacred mystery.

Not all can be known. Not all will be known.

Paradoxes offer seeds of new growth for the nomadic journey.

"WESTERN CHRISTIANITY HAS TRIED FOR TOO LONG TO MAKE THE GOSPEL A KIND OF SCIENTIFIC FORMULA—A PSEUDOSCIENCE OF BIBLICAL FACTS, ATONEMENT THEORIES, AND SINNERS' PRAYERS—WHEN IT IS MORE LIKE A SONG, A SYMPHONY, A POEM, A PAINTING, A DRAMA, A DANCE, AND, YES, A MYSTERY. ROOM FOR MYSTERY IS NECESSARY FOR ORTHODOX THEOLOGY. MYSTERY IS GOOD FOR THEOLOGY. AND MYSTERY IS GOOD FOR THE SOUL."[1] — BRIAN ZAHND

Allowing a sense of mystery to be part of our faith was something far more common in the Church's past. The culture of the Evangelical Church in America has sought to reduce that which cannot be fully proved, known, or understood. "Since the Enlightenment, an emphasis on reason has taken hold of the Western imagination. 'If you cannot reason or verbalize it, it must not be real, or true.' Thus, if you cannot understand something about your faith, it might cause a faith crisis."[2] But we have now entered a different chapter of the church. "Karl Rahner, a German Catholic priest, and theologian predicted that the Christian of the future will be a mystic or nothing at all. By 'mystic' we simply mean a person who seeks, and at some level attains *a direct experience within the mystery of God.*"[3]

THE HISTORY OF THE CHURCH INCLUDES THOSE WHO ALLOWED MYSTERY TO BE PART OF THEIR KNOWING OF GOD.

These recognized that *not* all can be known, and that often there must be a spiritual appraisal of truth, beyond intellect alone. We know them to be the mystics, they include names like Francis of Assisi, Julian of Norwich, Teresa of Avila, St. John of the Cross, and Thomas Merton. Many of these names are now re-appearing on bookshelves today, as mystics help lead us into a journey of seeing and knowing more of our God.

Even though I acknowledge the value of the mystics, I can still find myself agreeing with Parker Palmer when he says: "It is so much easier to deal with the external world, to spend our lives manipulating people and institutions, or fixing the lives of others and things, rather than dealing with our own souls. We like to talk about the outer world as if it was infinitely complex and demanding, but it is a cakewalk compared to the labyrinth of our souls."[4]

But it is the souls of many that hunger for more who have become unlikely nomads.

They have gone through the painful separation from their local church because there exists deep within, a genuine hunger for more in their life with Jesus. Their souls cry out for a deeper level of journey with Jesus. Over the last forty years, local churches re-positioned their ministries to meet the needs of those who were new in their faith. Going deeper was left to the individual to find on their own. While it is true that nomads are on a journey to a new church, for many that means a deeper, spiritual journey with Jesus, lived out in an authentic, spiritual community.

In the initial stages of our formation in Christ, we often feel and experience God's transforming love in real, tangible ways. But there comes a season, especially in the second half of our journey with Christ, when things begin to change. When the issues move away from the basics of faith, and onto issues of deeper, spiritual formation. This is the moment when we encounter far more questions than answers. It also is when the voice of Jesus appears to go faint. All our normal tools and attempts to draw closer to him seem to fail. Christ-followers often feel isolated, and unable to keep moving forward in their faith. The ancients of the faith tell us that this moment is often known as the *Dark Night of the Senses*, or the *Dark Night of the Soul.* It is when we realize that the issue is not whether Jesus is still speaking, but how badly we want to hear his voice. In the beginning, God chases us, but there comes a time when *we must chase him*.

Many nomads are at this moment and season in their formation. And it is often the mysteries of our faith that now need to be acknowledged, and included in the journey. When we accept that not everything we believe is based on reason and intellect, but rather on faith and an acceptance of that which is not known, and yet we believe, it is an acknowledgment of paradoxes that are part of our faith. They are even employed as we go deeper into the mystery of a God who deeply loves us. It is also that moment in time, when new practices must replace yesterday's habits. The maturing of our faith often requires a shift in our paradigms, and how we see God, self, and others. Finishing well will not occur unless we are willing to journey through a series of paradigm shifts, and paradoxes, that will need to be embraced.

Four mysteries of faith, yield four paradoxes that have surfaced over the last thirty years of my personal journey, and used by the Spirit to take my faith to a new place. They have also re-appeared as I have coached those who now seek lives more like Jesus, and often navigate around the church, in order to grow in their faith. It is likely that those who are unlikely nomads will bump into these core mysteries and paradoxes, as they walk new roads that lead to a life more like Jesus. The mysteries of *being, sovereignty, sacrifice,* and *grace* are more fully embraced as we confront four paradoxes:

- Being *and* doing
- Sovereignty *and* Responsibility
- Self-defined *and* Self-less
- Grace *and* Truth

PARADOXES

As a child, I remember visiting playgrounds comprised of just two apparatuses: swings and teeter-totters. It was the teeter-totters that always drew my attention. I would grab a playmate, and try to find that one point of balance, the fulcrum point of equal tension between both our sides. I loved it when we found the place where both sat suspended in mid-air, perfectly balanced. How it worked was a mystery to me as a young child, but all I knew was that when it did, grins and laughter would erupt on our faces. It was much more exciting than just swinging on a boring swing.

In a paradox, opposites do not negate—they balance each other, both offering truth and contribution to a moment in time that could not be achieved separately. How both sides of a paradox can be true, at the same time, is the mystery and the agent of change. Together, they cause our lives to be something far more because they each reveal the way we grow as we seek to live in the Kingdom of heaven, here on earth.

Just as the body requires both breathing *in* and breathing *out*, a paradox presents two parts of one truth, and serves to sustain our spiritual lives. It is often far easier to favor one side over the other, but both are essential. The strange twist is that the more we embrace what we do not understand, the greater the potential for growth, and deeper understanding. Though we may never allow ourselves to confess this truth publicly, all of us have far more questions about our faith, than answers. The embracing of the paradoxes and mysteries of the faith is the seedbed for more honest and authentic faith. It is core to the journey of nomads.

LET'S REVISIT THE FOUR PARADOXES I INTRODUCED ABOVE AND EXPLORE THE WAYS THEY PROMOTE NEW GROWTH.

The Paradox of Being and Doing ... embracing the cultivation of the inner life, while at the same time, actively engaging in living out the life of Jesus. It can sound like this when we confront this paradox:

> *Do I spend my days going deeper in my journey with Jesus, trying new practices, and focusing on my interior development? Or, do I step out, serving Christ in new ways, and intentionally invest time in loving my neighbors and my community?*

The answer is *yes*. It is a call to integrate deeper intimacy with new behaviors that better match the life of Jesus. Our first order is the call to be. Our second order is the call to do. The communion we share within the Trinity is what empowers our lives in Christ. Jesus' mission and life were wrapped within his ongoing communion with the Father (and Spirit). Jesus knew what was ahead of him each day as a result of his daily communion with the Father (John 5:19-20).

NOMADIC LIVES ...

In the days ahead, nomads must develop regular times of disengagement from the culture, and times of being with Jesus, before re-engagement with the culture can become meaningful. Natural abilities, past experiences, or acquired skills will not suffice, or provide strength to meet the challenges ahead. Living in the tension of being and doing is critical.

The Paradox of Absolute Sovereignty and Human Responsibility ... embracing the truth that God is sovereign, and possesses the right to determine the future, while at the same time, we each assume personal responsibility to live out each day in obedience to Christ. It can sound like this when we confront the paradox:

> *Do I just sit back and wait for God to move, and the new church to emerge? Or, am I supposed to take responsibility for my actions, aligning with Christ, and engaging the issues all around me?*

The answer once again is *yes*. Knowing that God is in control, provides the platform to live out the life of Jesus, demonstrating our trust in him through obedience. This paradox requires that the nomadic journey must be one of daily surrendering our desires to his control. We are called to play our part in our growth, trust, and dependence on his sovereign, shaping work.

NOMADIC LIVES ...

Remember Peter's response when Jesus asked if he and the other disciples would abandon the new work that had begun? "Lord, to whom shall we go? You have the words of eternal life" (John 6:68). To follow Jesus in the days ahead, nomads will be called on to accept the Shepherd's leading, and choose to follow him completely, though the destination will be unclear.

The Paradox of Self-defined and Self-less ... embracing a sense of clear, personal identity, accepting who God has shaped us to be, while at the same time living a self-less life, sacrificial and ready to respond to a given need. It can sound like this when we confront this paradox:

> *Should I work on clarifying my personal identity in Christ, knowing that boundaries are vital, and knowing who I am/am not? Or, should I not worry about stepping over lines and sacrificing myself for the sake of the Gospel?*

Once again, our answer is *yes* to both, not one or the other. The notion of being "self-defined" is one of the most important concepts to which nomads must subscribe. Thomas Merton said: "This is not the ego self that wants to inflate us ... not the intellectual self that wants to hover above the mess of life ... not the ethical self that wants to live by some abstract moral code. It is the [true] self-planted in us by the God who made us in God's own image."[5] In Mark 9:35, Jesus proclaimed: "Anyone who wants to be first must be the very last, and the servant of all."

NOMADIC LIVES...

Nomads are called to a new understanding of self. Neither one of independence nor one of dependence. But rather one of inter-dependence. One that will take intentional choice and practice. It will be best lived out in the context of community.

The Paradox of Grace and Truth ... embracing the paradox of non-judgment and offering grace to all we meet, while at the same time walking with integrity, and living out the faith we profess, speaking truth as the measurement of one's life. It can sound like this when we confront this paradox:

> *God, how do I offer grace, and share your love and acceptance of all people, especially in light of issues that now polarize the world we live in? And what does it look like when I share truth and yet seek to stay consistent with the grace you offer?*

"THE WORD BECAME FLESH AND MADE HIS DWELLING AMONG US. WE HAVE SEEN HIS GLORY, THE GLORY OF THE ONE AND ONLY SON, WHO CAME FROM THE FATHER, FULL OF GRACE AND TRUTH" — JOHN 1:14

The life of Jesus models for us that grace and truth can travel together. A focus on truth alone brings with it a judgmental attempt to discern another's motives, which is often impossible. Grace alone can mean a Gospel that looks past all acts and behaviors. Jesus stood in a circle that surrounded a woman, each ready to stone her, and declared that all in the circle were the same as this woman. It is the moment when we separate ourselves and hide our own sin, that hypocrisy grows. One distinction of Christianity, over other religions of the world, is the concept of grace. Most religious individuals want to experience grace, but make sure others are held accountable to truth.

NOMADIC LIVES ...

This paradox can only be truly lived out by nomads who are willing to be misunderstood. When you offer both grace and truth, not everyone will understand or agree. "It sometimes seems that for each thing we sought, we have found not only that which we searched for, but also its opposite."[6]

Adopting the reality of mysteries and paradoxes, almost feels contradictory, in and of itself. But, embracing both sides of a truth can offer new hope, and return us back to the life that Christ lived. To believe, and hold truths in tension, especially those which seem opposite in focus, digs deeper wells. Jesus came announcing a very different type of Kingdom. The Kingdom of *Heaven* was at hand. One comprised of fewer absolutes than we sometimes proclaim. Living out the life of his Kingdom will forge a different kind of church, and is worthy of the nomadic journey ahead.

CHAPTER TWENTY-ONE

FIRST FRUITS

I leave you with some first fruits.

Initial tastes of what could be ahead, and a new kind of church. But first, a quick excursion through wine country.

Robin and I live in Northern California.

We love to venture to the California Coast and visit the wine country. So many vineyards now populate the coast, way beyond just the Napa Valley region. So much to explore, and so little time. Wine tasting, up and down the coast, with friends, is time worth savoring. We are neither wine experts, nor claim to be part of the wine elite. But, with each new wine-tasting adventure, we have grown in our recognition of the various types of grapes and wine. They say that the more you sample the various varieties and blends of wine, the more your *palette* expands, and the greater you can recognize the value of the wine. Though our goal remains enjoying the adventure, and spending time with good friends, the farther we go down the back roads and hills covered with new vines, the more we marvel at all that is now a part of the landscape, often out of sight of those who travel the main highways. *New vineyards producing new wine.*

This analogy is too good not to include.

On the back roads, and hidden hillsides, new vineyards have been planted, over the landscapes of America. As the vines have matured over time, they now are yielding grapes that are being turned into new wine. Though these vineyards still remain unknown to many, new wine has been aging in the barrels, and is now ready to be sampled. The more visitors sample this new wine, the more the word spreads of its richness and value. Years before, planting, cultivating, and pruning occurred. Once harvested, there were times of crushing, and pressing. And then, time to age. Out in the vineyards, those who sample this new wine pass by others who have traveled many roads to find these vineyards. This new wine is a result of a new breed of winemakers.

**JESUS WAS CLEAR.
WHEN THERE IS NEW WINE,
WE NEED NEW WINESKINS.**

"And no one pours new wine into old wineskins. Otherwise, the new wine will burst the skins; the wine will run out and the wineskins will be ruined. No, new wine must be poured into new wineskins" (Luke 5:37-38).

The *Joshuas* and *Calebs* of our day are bringing back accounts of the new wine, and the new wineskins that are being fashioned. As I have coached and listened to their stories, I have recognized that:

- The taste of the new wine resembles the varieties found in the days of early harvest, and the calling of the first apprentices of Jesus. The first of the new wineskins were often experienced in smaller authentic communities, practicing the presence of Jesus together. These smaller communities allowed for greater depth and growth.

- The character of this new wine comes from vines that have been deeply embedded in the rugged terrain of the hillsides. Their time spent in these sunbaked soils has yielded a different variety of grapes; bolder, and a richer, more authentic expression of the Gospel than we have known before.
- The richness of the new wine is coming from a deeper formation ... one that is the by-product of intentional, ongoing sharing and development. It is wine that is the result of a defined journey from vineyard to glass, as opposed to a quick-fix, rush to market. It is the fruit of God's shaping of lives, and surrender to his deepening work.
- And maybe best of all, this new wine is not the first fruits of vineyards run by the experts or famous labels, but workers like you and me ... normal, average workers, a priesthood of all believers, out in the vineyards. These same workers often gather together, right out in the vineyard, for a meal, time together, and the sharing of life.

BRIDGING CHURCHES

If you have made it this far in the book, you may have said (more than once):

> *"But Terry, you don't know our church. We do all that you are talking about, and more. I believe we are a church for nomads!"*

There are good churches living out Jesus' call to make disciples.

They are seeking to apprentice new disciples for a new kind of church. Hallelujah! And these churches are part of the new work Jesus is doing in the local churches of America. I call these *Bridging Churches.*

Bridging Churches are local churches committed to the new ways in which Jesus is at work in his church. They have come to terms with the reality that the church is transitioning to a new chapter. Though they continue in a form similar to past expressions of the local church, these are led by leaders who recognize the need for the church that exists, to be a *bridge* into a new expression of the church. They seek to equip Christ-followers to express the church in new ways, beyond Sunday church. They promote experimentation, and new ways to join mission and discipleship. *These churches have given the church back to Jesus.* They have moved the church out on the fringe, into neighborhoods, front yards, urban spaces, marketplaces, campuses, pubs, and beyond.

Calvary Church in State College, Pennsylvania (mentioned earlier) is one such church.

Even though it is based in Pennsylvania, my wife and I, who live in Chico, CA, attend Calvary. I know that just set off alarms within some, but we have been to Calvary many times, and are aligning with their commitment to front-yard missions, and becoming a bridging church into the future. Though State College, PA and Chico, CA are miles apart, our towns are both university towns. Each week, we attend the online services, where we are equipped and share in times of communion, right in our living room. Our desire is to better know how to apprentice the life of Jesus in our neighborhood. Calvary helps us build bridges with our neighbors. We do share accountability with other believers. There are hundreds of Bridging Churches out there. Ones that you can connect to, and who can help you find and gather with those in your neighborhood.

EMBEDDED COMMUNITIES

These are expressions of community, and the apprenticing of Jesus where 2-4 families are either already present or chose to move into local neighborhoods to live the life of Jesus, together. They seek to create environments where people can gather and more intentionally experience the dynamics of *life together*. These expressions seek to counteract the limited community that comes when believers just *attend* small groups or church services. In these communities, meals, mission, relationships, and sometimes even economics are done together. They often join in a covenant to experience the ways of Jesus, together. In places like Portland, St. Paul, and San Diego those committed to this form of community, share in mission, learning, and the call to justice and healing. They often focus on issues of sustainability, unique local needs, and offer co-op approaches to basic issues like food, clothing, the environment, and more.

COMMONS

Growing numbers of new expressions have begun shifting the focus off of a *Sunday-morning centric* approach, and now see daily connection and interactions around a *common* community meeting place. Many neighborhoods and urban dwelling spaces see a coffee spot and community center as common ground. These are distinguished from a local church and mission outreach. These are gathering points for multi-generational nomad types, who gather to cultivate genuine relationships with like-minded apprentices of Jesus, across a wide spectrum of individuals. While the design and function of the places are varied, they offer a safe-place for daily conversations and connection. Business types, entrepreneurs, and new moms feel welcomed with their young families. Commons often become the initial meeting place that serves to ignite future meals together, block parties, and talks around the fire pit. Though their forms are all different, they are places of informal gatherings for those who have tired of the institutional meetings, and who hunger for the exchange of life, together.

STORE FRONTS

Across the American landscape, new places of commerce and community are surfacing, linking together Kingdom-minded nomads, local enterprises, and the offering of services that meet the needs of a local community. They are working spaces, coffee shops, second-hand apparel shops, restaurants, pubs, public gardens, etc. These serve the immediate context, but also can be linked globally, to new initiatives and markets. They are often the combined dream of spiritual entrepreneurs and community architects, who combine to create new spaces that facilitate connection and new Kingdom initiatives. *Storefronts* move the church beyond the limits of one-time-use buildings, and expand the potential of Kingdom life and enterprise. It is the church in the marketplace. They are places where emerging young leaders often flourish.

MICRO CHURCHES

Micro churches offer minimal structure and the connecting of small gatherings of Christ-followers to function as a viable organic expression of church community. Their organization tends to be flat, they are much more egalitarian, and they offer much more flexibility as Jesus' apprentices share a passion for a local community.

Micro churches typically have no paid clergy. They minister one to the other, with an emphasis on the life of Jesus expressed together. Their interest is not that of numbers, or repeating what happens in the typical, Sunday church service. Rather, they seek deeper community as they share the sacraments. One distinguishing hallmark is their linkage to other micro churches. They have both accountability and ongoing resourcing that comes from being a part of a network of micro churches. *The Underground Network* in the Tampa Bay, Florida area is such a network of over 200 local, micro churches. They share extended community and mission, and have built a platform where resources and services can be exchanged across a vast array of needs.

COLLECTIVES

The *Parish Collective* connects people who desire to see church be part of a neighborhood. This collective serves those throughout the U.S. who see the neighborhood as a defined parish, by offering gathering events that convene neighborhood expressions for community and resourcing. *Collectives* typically bring together those in a geographic place large enough to be known for the story of a certain place. The connection occurs as people share their stories of lessons learned and by celebrating ordinary heroes. They bring people together either online or in-person for shared learning and inspiration, through gatherings and learning communities. Collectives believe that when they organize the expression of church around God's dreams for their neighborhoods, there is nothing in the world that cannot be healed, transformed, and liberated.

"THEREFORE, SINCE WE ARE RECEIVING A KINGDOM THAT CANNOT BE SHAKEN, LET US BE THANKFUL, AND SO WORSHIP GOD ACCEPTABLY WITH REVERENCE AND AWE, FOR OUR 'GOD IS A CONSUMING FIRE.'" — HEBREWS 12:28-29

AS I FINISH THE WRITING OF THIS BOOK ...

We are still in close proximity to the time when the Spirit moved in on the student prayer meetings at Asbury College, in Willmore Kentucky. Though the meetings have now subsided, the unexpected outpouring of the Spirit on the students of that campus, spread to other university campuses in the U.S. It was reminiscent of the similar occurrence that occurred at Asbury College back in the 70s, which coincided with all that was happening on the West coast with The Jesus Movement in Southern California. A breaking in of the Spirit that I experienced (see chapter three). These become moments of hope that often signal a coming change.

Stirrings. Rumblings. Moments in time when Aslan is on the move. We who are alive today have witnessed a seismic shift in the structures of our world, and the decline of the local church in America.

THERE IS NO GOING BACK TO NORMAL, BECAUSE NORMAL NO LONGER EXISTS.

It is in the crushing … and in the pressing … that new wine is produced.

New wine is fermenting in places as distinct as England, China, Iraq, Africa, and the United States. New wine, and new wineskins, are surfacing even in oppressive regimes of our world, and where the church once was strong. The next chapter of the church has begun.

When Jesus arrived on the scene, his life and message announced that a new Kingdom had come. It threatened the religious, shook the skeptics, shattered the pre-conceptions of those waiting for a Messiah, and ignited a movement of those hungering for a new move of God. That which appeared to be unshakable, has once again been shaken. Like in those early moments, nomads are once again dropping their nets and following Jesus. And though the destination is unclear, they have heard the voice of the Shepherd, and they have packed their bags, and left. Jesus is at work, leading his church to someplace new.

He himself told us that the presence of new wine would mean the need for new wine skins.

It's time to go.

ARE YOU COMING?

APPENDIX

TRANSITION ESSENTIALS

EXCERPTS FROM THE LEADER BREAKTHRU TRANSITIONS BOOK SERIES

Stuck!, Awakening, Deciding, Finishing
by Terry B. Walling

"So much of this life is lived in between, between the now and the not yet, between arriving and departing, between growing up and growing old, between questions and answers. Lord, help us not to live for the distant day when the in-between will be no more, but help us to have the courage to step into that sacred space of the in-between—knowing that this is a place where life is transformed."

—JIM BRANCH, *THE BLUE BOOK*

"Every transition begins with an ending. We have to let go of the old thing before we can pick up the new—not just outwardly, but inwardly."

—WILLIAMS BRIDGES, *MANAGING TRANSITIONS*

TRANSITIONS ARE REAL

"Terry, you've got to help me out! Something's all wrong! I don't know what's happening."

"Okay, slow down" I responded. "Tell me what's up, Daniel. What's going on?"

"I don't know what's going on! That's the point. I don't know if I'm confused, depressed, lazy, or all three. Am I losing it? I don't know where I am anymore, and I have no clue where I'm going."

"What brought all of this on?" I asked. "I know things have been tough, but the last time we talked, you seemed to feel like you were on track." "I know," he replied. "But now I wonder if I've been off for some time now. No matter what I try, nothing seems to get any better. And worst of all, God has gone silent. I thought I was doing what God wanted me to, but I feel like I've completely lost the plot."

"Slow down," I responded, as calmly as possible. "And let's walk our way back through this together. It sounds like there's more going on here than just a bad week!"

Daniel and I then proceeded to walk back through his past and then forward through months of fog and uncertainty that had clearly descended on his life. Step by step, we trudged through self-doubt, questions of adequacy, and fears that somehow he had gotten things wrong in terms of knowing what God wanted.

The real problem wasn't that Daniel had gotten it wrong, but, rather, the more he tried to sort it all out, the more his paralysis spread. Every door he tried to pry open to help answer his confusion proved to be yet another dead end. Daniel was stuck.

Daniel and his wife are among the best and most gifted Christ-followers I know. Long ago, they had surrendered their lives to the control of Jesus Christ and they had followed their King to the front lines of Christian ministry. Somehow, we can let ourselves get trapped into thinking that our best and brightest are beyond these moments of feeling lost. But that's not true.

No matter how mature one may be as a Christian, a person can only handle so much frustration, confusion, and lack of direction before he or she begins to lose hope. Daniel had done all the right things, yet answers from God seemed to move further and further away. I was beginning to hear and feel a loss of resolve seeping into his voice as we continued our coaching relationship over the phone. Behind him was a place where he knew he couldn't return to in his spiritual growth, but ahead of him was a path for the next chapter with God that was both unknown and uncertain.

Daniel was on a pilgrimage of character that all Christ-followers must face from time to time. It was much more than merely a period of frustration or things not going his way. Instead, Daniel had entered a defining moment in his development as a leader and Christ follower called a transition. Without exception, every committed Christ-follower and leader will be called to travel this same road.

But, as he traveled, Daniel had hit a danger moment in his transition.

The endless loop of frustration and confusion had taken its toll. He was close to the edge of losing the new ministry God had for him. From the outside, I could see a trap was being set. His weariness and confusion were being used by the enemy to lure

Daniel away from all that God was intending to do within him. Like so many before him, Daniel wanted an easy fix or a shortcut to a deeper, true work of God.

Many committed Christ-followers have jumped off-road as a result of times like these. Short-circuited transitions have led to times of plateau, arrested development, and even walking away from the faith.

Who doesn't want to fast-forward to the good stuff? Who doesn't want hope more than confusion and to live in victory as opposed to apparent failure? However noble we may each look on the outside, we've all flirted with how we might quietly skip the hard stuff.

Our many books and workshops often serve to fuel those shortcut desires. *Type A* individuals are especially at risk. They typically want to "cut to the chase," get to the finish line, and forgo the mess of wandering deeper into the processing fog. Whatever your personality type, we all hit those moments when enough is enough.

Transitions occur in the lives of business people, vocational ministers, homemakers, students, young and old, church and non-churched alike. For Christ-followers, something more is occurring—something more than just a change in career direction or the need for new scenery. God does some of His most important formation during the transition times of His followers. He sculpts life purpose and direction during the in-between times of our lives.

Transitions aren't new. Transitions pushed Moses onward, moving him beyond his doubts and inadequacies. A major transition occurred in Joshua's life that thrust him into a major role of leadership, taking the Israelites into the Promise Land. It was a series of life transitions that transformed a fisherman named Peter into an apostolic leader of the early church.

Transitions were also used to advance the lives and leadership roles of Bonhoeffer, Wesley, and Moody, along with more contemporary figures like Graham, Bright, and Warren. Each of those who have gone before us have experienced major times of in-between: times full of uncertainty and questions en route to living lives that please God. Transitions are also occurring in the lives of people like you and me.

They happen every day among faithful followers of Jesus: moms, kids, friends, brothers and sisters, work associates, and more all experience transitions. God uses transitions to both deepen and widen the influence of those who choose to love Christ with their lives.

It was nearly two years later when I received a phone message from Daniel. The recorded cell phone update was short, clear, and enthusiastic: "Hey, Walling! I've had a breakthrough. I see what's next and what God is at work doing! Don't coach me any more about this in-between, transition stuff. God is speaking again! Hallelujah! Call me if you want to know more."

TRANSITIONS ARE DIFFERENT

"WE SPEND MOST OF OUR LIVES TRYING TO MAKE THINGS HAPPEN FOR OURSELVES, AND FOR THE PEOPLE WE LOVE. BUT LIFE CANNOT BE REDUCED TO WHAT YOU GIVE OR KNOW OR ACHIEVE. LIFE IS NOT REDUCED TO YOUR MISTAKES, YOUR FAILURES, OR YOUR SIN. LIFE ISN'T EVEN DEFINED BY WHOM YOU LOVE. RATHER, IT IS DE- FINED BY THE GOD WHO LOVES YOU."
—M. CRAIG BARNES, *SACRED THIRST*

A transition is an in-between period in the life development of a Christ-follower. In a transition, individuals consolidate past learning, process issues of character, deepen convictions and values, and are prepared for the next phase of their development. Transitions bring closure to the past in order to move forward to the next stage of personal development.

Transitions are characterized by a prolonged period of restlessness, self-doubt, lack of motivation, stagnation, diminished confidence, lack of direction, distance from God, isolation, relational conflict and tension, lack of effectiveness, and a struggle to stay focused and motivated.

You may currently feel some of these traits on a regular basis. But with a transition, characteristics like these persist over a prolonged period of time.

Another way to recognize a transition is the realization of the deeper work that God is doing. Transitions are more about character development than job description. In a transition, God turns a searchlight on the heart.

TRANSITIONS ARE OFTEN FILLED WITH FAR MORE QUESTIONS THAN ANSWERS—QUESTIONS SUCH AS:

- Why have I lost my passion?
- Why can't I shake this restlessness?
- Why do I feel isolated?
- Why all the inconsistencies?
- Why all the inconsistencies?
- Why do I keep rehearsing tapes from the past?
- What would happen if I do step out?
- What if I fail?

SELF-DEFINITION

God uses transitions to help followers press into greater clarity about who they are. Self-knowledge is essential for emotional health and for coming to terms with one's unique contribution. God uses transitions to help Christ-followers discover who they are, but also who they aren't. For these reasons, transitions often include struggles with self-confidence, relational tensions with family and friends, feelings of self-worth and a lack of acceptance, and struggles with fear and personal inadequacy.

ROLE

Role is about more than one's job. Role has to do with contribution. Over a lifetime, God desires to bring to the surface the good works that He has authored for all Christ-followers (Ephesians 2:10). Each person is gifted to make an impact. Transitions bring clarity to the working together of one's abilities, skills, and spiritual gifts. Role clarifies contribution in the church, on the job, and in your family and community. For these reasons, transitions often include ongoing frustrations over effectiveness, continued struggle with job fit, and restlessness over passion and contribution. A hunger grows to not just live a life of busy work.

PARADIGMS

Transitions also bring to the surface the need for new knowledge and necessary changes in one's paradigms. In order to move forward, each Christ-follower needs to think in new ways, as well as achieve greater clarity in one's knowledge base. Lifelong learning is one key to finishing well. A breakthrough in worldview often comes with new opportunities and options. For these reasons, transitions often include challenges to one's presuppositions, disturb plateaus in growth, bring to the surface the need for education and training, and create an internal restlessness for a deeper journey with God.

Going through transitions is about God having the right to be God. Transitions forge new trust. Without transitions, we would slide into a malaise of the same and stop growing. Because of this, God allows the difficult, the confusing, and even the hurtful to enter a life—not because of His lack of caring, but to take us deeper into our pursuit of Him.

What makes this issue of greater relevance and impact today is the unprecedented, global change that now drives life into a time of perpetual transition. The speed of change is throwing fuel upon the intensity already present in transitions.

This overview is fleshed out in greater detail in my book *Stuck! Navigating the Transitions of Life and Leadership*. It offers a more in-depth understanding of the purpose of a transition, a Transition Life Cycle that provides you a road map for how transitions often occur. It also provides insights into the three, strategic transitions, and four 'looks' that can help you to more deeply process a transition. *Stuck!* also includes coaching questions and a small group outline to help you process the idea of transitions with others.

In *Stuck!* I also identify three major, strategic transitions that all Christ-followers will go through. These three transitions are the basis for three additional books I have written, one of each of these critical moments of in-between.

Awakening is first of these transition moments (and books), often occurring in the lives of those in their 20s-late 30s. This transition is foremost a call to experience Christ and a life of intimacy with him before it is a call to do work for him. It is a call "to" someone, before it is a call to "do" something. The focus of the Awakening Transition is that of direction, identity, and personal calling.

The ***Deciding Transition*** can often occur somewhere in a leader's early-40s to mid-50s. This transition introduces to those in the mid-stage of life issues of Major Role, Effective Methods and recognizing the need to say 'no' in order to say 'yes' to how God has shaped each of our lives. The focus of the Deciding Transition is that of clarifying a Christ-followers unique, Kingdom Contribution,

There is no such thing as "retirement." ***The Finishing Transition*** does not mean you are finished. There is important influence and contribution still ahead. This often occurs somewhere in an individual's in their 60s to late-70s, and introduce you to issues of convergence, finishing well. And influence and impact without position.

YOU CAN FIND EACH OF THESE RESOURCES AND MORE AT, LEADERBREAKTHRU.COM/STORE

ACKNOWLEDGMENTS

This book has been different from the others I have written that focused on lifelong development and the coaching of leaders. This one has been personal. Putting into words more than thirty years of ministry lessons was no easy task.

THIS BOOK OCCURRED AS A RESULT OF TWO INDIVIDUALS:

My son, Kyle, who prefers to be out of the limelight, yet *Unlikely Nomads* is in your hands because of his efforts in helping me translate my thoughts and impressions, into more precise words and a readable design. He has done this for me for more than twenty years, and I am eternally grateful for who he is, even more than all the skills he employed to help bring my lifework to print.

My friend, Leslyn Musch, is both my greatest cheerleader, and final editor. Together, she and Kyle helped me push *Unlikely Nomads* over the finish line. She, and husband Ron, have been a source of great encouragement in terms of the need for this book. Leslyn not only brought key suggestions to the text, but also needed refinements to the manuscript. I am so thankful, Leslyn, for all your efforts in helping make this book into reality.

Lots of thanks and love to *Robin* for her perseverance with me through this two year effort, along with friends and comrades that have believed in me, and shared a like-passion for Kingdom leaders; *Joel and Grace Lam, Elaine May, Nick In't Hout, Randy Gonzalez, Kim Zovak, Dan Nold, Rob and Laurie Yackley, Kevin Abbott, Mark Sayers, Peter Woods, Jim and Linda Porter, Josh Lindblom,* and too many others I am not remembering as I write.

NOTES

INTRODUCTION + CHAPTER ONE

[1] Tim Keller, "Tim Keller on the Decline and Renewal of the American Church," *The Gospel Coalition*, February 20, 2023, https://www.thegospelcoalition.org/article/tim-keller-decline-renewal-american-church/

[2] Henri Nouwen, *The Way of the Heart* (Seabury Press, 1981), p. 77

[3] Mark Sayers, *A Non-anxious Presence* (Chicago: Moody Press, 2022), p. 26

[4] Dietrich Bonhoeffer, *Life Together* (Minneapolis: Fortress Press, 2015), p. 76

[5] William Bridges, *Managing Transitions* (Cambridge: Perseus Books, 1933), p. 4

[6] Chuck Girard, Maranatha Music ©1972

[7] Barna Research Group, "Two in Five Christians Are Not Engaged in Discipleship," January 26, 2022, https://www.barna.com/research/christians-discipleship-community/

[8] Barna Research Group, "Christians: More Like Jesus or Pharisees?" June 3, 2013, https://www.barna.com/research/christians-more-like-jesus-or-pharisees/

CHAPTER TWO

[1] Brian Zahnd, *Water to Wine,* (Spello Press, 2016), p.38

[2] Ibid., p. 38

[3] Adam Macinnis, "The Church is Losing its Grey Heads," *Christianity Today,* February 14, 2022, https://www.christianitytoday.com/ct/2022/march/gray-gen-x-boomers-older-churchgoers-leaving-church.html

[4] Ibid.

[5] Josh Packard and Ashleigh Hope, *Church Refugees* (Group Publishing, 2015), p. 38

[6] Kristin Kobes Du Mez, *Jesus and John Wayne,* (New York: Liveright Publishing, 2020), p. 99

[7] Ibid., p. 26

[8] *Merriam Webster Dictionary*

[9] Kristin Kobes Du Mez, *Jesus and John Wayne,* p. 26

[10] Willow Creek Pastor Greg L. Hawkins, Cally Parkison quoted from the Reveal Report, and cited in the blog: *Christian Leadership Alliance,* https://ym.christianleadershipalliance.org/page/revealed

[11] Ibid.

[12] Philip Yancey, *The Christian Paradox* (Grand Rapids: Zondervan, 2005), p. 41

CHAPTER THREE

[1] Janet Hagberg and Robert Guelph, *The Critical Journey* (Sheffield Publishing Company, 2005) p. 39

[2] Dr. J. Robert Clinton, *Leadership Emergence Manual,* (Pasadena: Barnabas Publishers, 1989), p. 130

[3] John H. Sammis, "Trust and Obey" (hymn), Public Domain

[4] George MacDonald, *Robert Falconer* (Wipf and Stock Publisher, 2012), p. 249, (quote is spoken by the character of Thomas Carlyle)

[5] Dr. J. Robert Clinton, *Leadership Emergence Manual,* p. 131

[6] Phyllis Tickle, *The Great Emergence,* (Grand Rapids: Baker Books, 2008), p. 16

[7] Ibid., p. 21

[8] Ibid., p. 20-21

[9] Ibid., p. 28

[10] Ibid., p. 28

CHAPTER FOUR

[1] J.R.R. Tolkien, *The Fellowship of the Ring* (George Allen & Unwin Publishers, 1954), Book 1, Chapter 1, p. 4

[2] E.A. Hoffman, "Leaning on the Everlasting Arms" (hymn), Public Domain

[3] Josh Packard & Ashley Hope, *Church Refugees* (Group Publishing, 2015), p. 74

CHAPTER FIVE

[1] C.S. Lewis, *The Collected Works of C.S. Lewis, Christian Reflections* (World Publishing, 1996), p.287

[2] Ruth Haley Barton, *Sacred Rhythms* (Downers Grove, IL: InterVarsity Press, 2022), p. 19

[3] C.S. Lewis, *The Lion Witch and Wardrobe* (HarperCollins, 2002), p. 59

[4] Henri Nouwen, *The Way of the Heart* (Ballantine Books; Reissue edition, 1985), p. 37

[5] Eugene Peterson, *A Long Obedience in the Same Direction* (Colorado Springs: NavPress, 2000), p. 111

CHAPTER SIX

[1] "New Wine," Words and Music by Brooke Ligertwood © Hillsong Music Publishing

[2] Tim Keller, "Tim Keller on the Decline and Renewal of the American Church," *The Gospel Coalition*, February 20, 2023, https://www.thegospelcoalition.org/article/tim-keller-decline-renewal-american-church/

[3] Henry & Richard Blackaby, Claude King, *Experiencing God: Knowing and Doing the Will of God Member Book [Revised]* (Lifeway Press, 2007) p. 115

[4] Jan Hettinga, *Follow Me* (Colorado Springs: NavPress, 1996), p. 104

CHAPTER SEVEN

[1] Songwriters: Don Henley and Stanley Lynch, "Learn To Be Still" lyrics © Matanzas Music, Black Cypress Music

[2] Dallas Willard, *Renovation of the Heart* (Colorado Springs: NavPress, 2012), p. 12

[3] John Ortberg, *The Life You Always Wanted* (Grand Rapids: Zondervan, 2002), p. 84

[4] Henri Nouwen, *The Three Movements of Spiritual Life* (HarperCollins, 1975), p. 124

[5] Ibid., p. 10

[6] Richard Foster, *Celebration of Discipline* (HarperOne, 1978), p. 87

[7] Henri Nouwen, Out of Solitude (Ave Maria Press, 2004), p. 22

[8] Stephen R. Covey, *The 7 Habits of Highly Effective People* (Simon & Shuster, 1989), p. 149

CHAPTER EIGHT

[1] Brian McClaren, *Faith After Doubt* (St. Martin's Essentials, 2021), p. 8

[2] *Encyclopedia Britianica*, clergy: https://www.britannica.com/topic/clergy-Christianity

[3] The International Astronomical Union (IAU), Astronomy for the Public, Definition of Dwarf Planet: https://www.iau.org/public/themes/pluto/

[4] Tim Keller, "American Christianity Is Due for a Revival," *The Atlantic,* February 5, 2023, https://www.theatlantic.com/ideas/archive/2023/02/christianity-secularization-america-renewal-modernity/672948/

[5] Mark Sayers, *Non-Anxious Presence,* List of Accepted Assumptions, p. 135

CHAPTER NINE

1 C.S. Lewis, *The Weight of Glory, and Other Addresses* (Macmillan, 1980), p. 26

2 Brian Zahnd, Article: "God is Like Jesus," August 11, 2011, https://brianzahnd.com/2011/08/god-is-like-jesus-2/

3 Mark Batterson, *All In* (Grand Rapids: Zondervan, 2013), p. 16

4 Parker Palmer, *A Hidden Wholeness* (Jossey-Bass, 2004), p. 20

5 Rich Villodas, *The Deeply Formed Life*, (WaterBrook, 2021), p. xxiv

6 James H. Cone, *The Cross and the Lynching Tree* (Orbis, 2011), p. iiiv

7 David Van Biema, "Mother Teresa's Crisis of Faith," Time Magazine, August 23, 2007, https://time.com/4126238/mother-teresas-crisis-of-faith

CHAPTER TEN

1 Rachel Held Evans, *Searching for Sunday* (Nashville: Thomas Nelson, 2015), p. 111

2 Tod Bolsinger, *Canoeing the Mountains* (InterVarsity Press, 2015), p. 39

3 Edwin Friedman, *Failure of Nerve* (Seabury Books, 1999), p. 14

4 Dietrich Bonhoeffer, *Life Together* (Fortress Press, 2015), p. 55-56

CHAPTER ELEVEN

1 Hugh Halter, *Flesh* (David C. Cook, 2014), p. 140

2 Global Entrepreneurship Monitor, "2021/2022 United States Report," p.36, https://www.gemconsortium.org/economy-profiles/united-states-2

3 Hugh Halter, *BiVO: A Modern-Day Guide for Bi-Vocational Saints* (Kindle, 2014), Loc 89-90

4 Hugh Halter & Matt Smay, *The Tangible Kingdom,* (Jossey-Bass, 2008), p 25

CHAPTER TWELVE

1 Shauna Niequist, *Bread & Wine* (Grand Rapids: Zondervan, 2013) p. 10

2 NT Wright, *Interpreting Scripture: Essays on the Bible and Hermeneutics* (Grand Rapids: Zondervan Academic, 2020), p. 349

CHAPTER THIRTEEN

[1] James H. Cone, *The Cross and the Lynching Tree* (Orbit Books, 2019), p. iiiv

[2] Ibid., p.28

[3] Jim Wallis, *America's Original Sin* (Baker Publishing, 2016), p. 173

CHAPTER FOURTEEN

[1] Dietrich Bonhoeffer, *Life Together* (SCM Press, 1972), p. 10

[2] Jon Huckins with Rob Yackley, *Thin Places* (The House Studio, 2012), p. 72

CHAPTER SIXTEEN

[1] Rosaria Champagne Butterfield, *The Gospel Comes with a House Key* (Crossway Books, 2018) p. 42

[2] Source: *Wikipedia*, https://en.wikipedia.org/wiki/Cape_St_George_Lighthouse

CHAPTER SEVENTEEN

[1] Wendell Berry, *Jayber Crow* (Counterpoint, 2001), p. 320-321

[2] Alan Hirsch, *5Q: Reactivating the Original Intelligence and Capacity of the Body of Christ* (100 Movements, 2017), p. 185

CHAPTER EIGHTEEN

[1] Mark Sayers, *Non-Anxious Presence,* p.108

[2] Lifeway Research, Article: "4 Reasons People Haven't Come Back to Church," June 7, 2023, https://research.lifeway.com/2023/06/07/4-reasons-people-havent-come-back-to-church

[3] Hugh Halter, taken from the Foreword (*Unlikely Nomads*, 2023)

[4] Richard Foster, *Revonaré,* Article: "Four Degrees of Love," https://renovare.org/articles/four-degrees-of-love

CHAPTER NINETEEN

[1] This quote is commonly attributed to Blaise Pascal, but it is not directly found in any of his published works. It is possible that he said the quote in a sermon or lecture, but there is no definitive source.

[2] Brené Brown, Article: "Creating Space," May 9, 2022, https://brenebrown.com/articles/2022/05/09/creating-space/

[3] Brother Lawrence, *The Practice of the Presence of God*, translated by E. M. Blaiklock (New York: HarperOne, 1992), p. 55

[4] Ibid., p. 19

[5] Ibid., p. 3

[6] Ibid., p. 24

[7] Ibid., p. 24-25

[8] *The Blue Book: A Devotional Guide for Every Season of Your Life* by Jim Branch is available at https://a.co/d/gbw0pCM

[9] Shelly Miller, *Rhythms of Rest* (Bethany House, 2016), p. 82

CHAPTER TWENTY

[1] Brian Zahnd, *Water to Wine* (Spello Press, 2016), p. 32

[2] Ibid, p. 31

[3] Brian Zahnd, *When Everything's on Fire* (Downers Grove, IL: InterVarsity Press, 2021), p. 125

[4] Parker Palmer, *Let Your Life Speak* (Jossey-Bass, 1999), p. 68-69

[5] Thomas Merton, *New Seeds of Contemplation*, (New Directions Publishing, 1961), p. 123.

[6] John Eldridge and Brent Curtis, *Sacred Romance* (Thomas Nelson, 1997), p. 149

ABOUT THE AUTHOR

Terry Walling is author of the best-selling book, *Stuck! Navigating the Transitions of Life and Leadership.* He coaches and consults ministry and marketplace Christ-followers who long to see that their lives count for the Kingdom of God.

Terry Walling is founder of Leader Breakthru, an innovative resourcing agency and ministry focused on coaching, creating breakthrough experiences and leadership development resources for risk-taking, Kingdom leaders. (leaderbreakthru.com)

Prior to founding Leader Breakthru, Terry served as Vice President with Church Resource Ministries (now Novo) in charge of its U.S. Ministries. He also served within CRM as Vice President for Church Revitalization.

Terry and Robin have been married for 40 years, and reside in Chico, California. He is a graduate of Point Loma College and Talbot Theological Seminary, and received his Doctor of Ministry in Global Ministry and Leadership Development from Fuller Theological Seminary.

Terry has taught in Doctor of Ministry programs in seminaries across North America in the area of Lifelong Leadership Development, and currently serves as Adjunct Professor at Fuller Theological Seminary, where he directs the Personal Mentoring and Coaching Cohort portion of their D.Min program.

TERRY HAS AUTHORED NUMEROUS BOOKS AND RESOURCES FOCUSED ON PERSONAL DEVELOPMENT AND RENEWAL, INCLUDING:

BOOKS

Stuck! Navigating Life and Leadership Transitions

Awakening: Awakening to the Call of God

Deciding: Clarifying Your Kingdom Contribution

Finishing: Completing the Race Set Before You

TRAC: Personalizing Personal Development

The IDEA Coaching Pathway: Coaching the Person (Instead of Just the Problem)

ONLINE COURSES & OTHER RESOURCES

Focused Living Online

Apex Online

Resonance Online

Perspective Workbook

Focus Workbook

Mentoring Workbook

Available at leaderbreakthru.com/store, or amazon.com

Made in the USA
Middletown, DE
02 March 2024

50695281R10154